Murders on Elderberry Road

A Queen Bees Quilt Mystery

by
Sally Goldenbaum

Murders on Elderberry Road
A Queen Bees Quilt Mystery

By Sally Goldenbaum

Editor: Steve Slack
Designer: Vicky Frenkel
Cover illustration: Neil Nakahodo
Character illustrations: Lon Eric Craven

Published by Kansas City Star Books.

First edition.

ISBN: 0-9740009-4-9
Library of Congress Control Number: 2003108440

Printed in the United States of America by Walsworth Publishing Co., Marceline, Missouri

To order copies, call StarInfo at (816) 234-4636 and say "BOOKS."

Order on-line at www.TheKansasCityStore.com.

STAR
BOOKS

Murders on Elderberry Road

A Queen Bees Quilt Mystery

◆

by
Sally Goldenbaum

KANSAS CITY STAR BOOKS

STAR
BOOKS

Acknowledgment

My thanks to Marnette Falley for introducing me to the world of quilting, for researching and designing the star quilt pattern, and for welcoming me into her Persian Pickles sewing group. Additional thanks to all the Pickles for sharing their amazing art and for their help in designing Selma's anniversary quilt. And a special thanks to Nancy Pickard — my mystery-writing mentor and muse — whose friendship, advice and encouragement made this book possible.

To Don, Todd, Aria, and Danny —
with great love.

PORTIA (PO) PALTROW,
founder and nurturer of the
Queen Bees quilting group.
Anchors the women's quilting
group in life and in art.

KATE SIMPSON,
Po's goddaughter and a
graduate student at the
college. The newest mem-
ber of the Queen Bees.

PHOEBE MELLON,
wife to Jimmy, an up-and-
coming lawyer, young mother
to eleven-month-old twins,
and a constant surprise to
her quilting cohorts.

ELEANOR CANTERBURY,
who lives on the edge of the
college her great-grandfather
founded. Is heir to the
Canterbury family fortune.

LEAH SARANDON,
professor of women's studies at Canterbury College. An artistic quilter.

SELMA PARKER,
owner of Parker's Dry Goods Store. Provides a weekly gathering place for the Queen Bees quilting group and generous doses of down-home wisdom.

SUSAN MILLER,
Selma's artistic assistant manager in the quilt shop. Recently returned to college to pursue a degree in fiber arts.

MAGGIE HELMERS,
Crestwood's favorite veterinarian. Is an avid quilter and collector of fat lady art.

◆

C H A P T E R   1

Sunshine & Shadow

Portia Paltrow stood at her back door and looked out into the thin, early light. She was getting a late start this morning. A brilliant autumn sun was already climbing into the sky, and in the distance Po could hear the familiar sounds of a town just beginning to wake up — the bark of a dog, the chug of a car engine, the sharp slap of the morning paper against the steps.

Po — as everyone called her — had had a busy week —

Sunshine & Shadow

1

two writing deadlines and several talks over at the college — and that extra hour of sleep had felt very fine. She wouldn't have the streets completely to herself at this later hour — there'd be plenty of co-eds jogging along the river, sleek and colorful in their bright Spandex, but Po could hold her own.

Turning sixty had found Po in better shape than she'd been twenty years earlier when children and PTAs and work had forced exercise and daily jogs onto the back burner. She smoothed a dab of sunscreen across her high cheekbones and down her nose, pressed a baseball cap onto her salt-and-pepper hair, and grabbed a plastic water bottle from the counter.

Po closed the door softly behind her — a habit born of living with Sam Paltrow for all those years. Sam had been a light sleeper, waking at the brush of a branch against their window screen or the sound of distant thunder, and for thirty-plus years Po had tiptoed through her precious early morning hours while Sam slept away the sunrise in snoreful bliss.

Curling her fingers around the side porch post, Po stretched the sleep from her arms and legs while early-morning thoughts of her Sam brought a smile to her lips. It was a good way to begin her run — with those thoughts of Sam. He loved that she jogged, loved that she returned sweaty and flushed and planted wet wakeup kisses on his sleeping forehead. Sam had loved everything about her, and she him. Po straightened up, tucked her memories back into her heart, and headed down the brick driveway and into the day.

Po relished the solitude that her morning jog afforded her — that quiet as soft as a baby's breath — which writing and three grandchildren often kept beyond her reach. She loved the smells, too, powerful in the early morning — sweet flowers in the spring, and the crisp, earthy aroma of fallen leaves and northern air in the fall. The quiet neighborhoods seemed to open up to her at this hour, and reminded her why she'd never leave this small college town, not after her Sam died and her sister tried to lure her to Florida; not now; and probably not ever, though Po was reluctant to think in finalities. And it wasn't just that she and Sam had shared a full life here — Po raising their kids and writing her books, Sam, the highly respected president of Canterbury College. And even now, with Sam gone, she loved her life here.

Po picked up speed — but not too much — and headed east, following the sun as it crept above the aging elms that lined the horizon like morning sentinels.

A short mile into her run, Po slowed her pace slightly and headed down the gravel alley that ran behind the Elderberry shops, a collection of small neighborhood stores that lined the sides of Elderberry Road. Sam had often joked that someday, when their bones started to creak and they couldn't drive anymore, they'd just hobble down to Elderberry for everything they needed — their books, their wine and cheese, and that extravagantly strong coffee that Marla had started making in her bakery café.

Sam always did have wonderful ideas. Maybe she'd just swing on back here on her way home — she'd buy a sack of Marla's sinful cinnamon rolls for her Queen Bees quilting group. Sam would have approved, and the women would love it.

Much like the nearby Emerald River, the alley curved like a slithering snake, this way and that, as did most streets in

Crestwood — no graph-paper-grid of streets found in most Midwest towns here. Po stayed close to the edge of the narrow gravel way. Sometimes there would be an early-morning delivery truck barreling through the narrow alley, scattering gravel every which way. They didn't stop for love nor money — and especially not for a sixty-year-old woman whose jog was more of a lope, whose ponytail was streaked with gray.

But today there was none of that. Today the alley was as quiet as a tomb with only the occasional squirrel darting out in front of her, staring her down, then scampering away as if he'd won some game he was playing with her. The strip of tall evergreens and euonymus bushes on Po's left hid the neighborhood houses and their large, toy-strewn yards. And to her right, the quiet bank of store backs, as familiar to her as her own name, was dark and still.

Po took note of the peeling paint beneath the eaves on Mary and Owen Hill's red brick antiques shop, Windsor House. Good grief — how embarrassed they'd be. She made a mental note to mention it to Owen. How that man managed everything he did, was beyond Po. He was chair of the art history department at Canterbury College — one of the best damn department heads he had, Sam always said. Owen traveled, lecturing at prestigious universities, helped run this elegant antique store, and even managed to entertain at his pastoral farm west of town. He was also on the board of ESOC, the Elderberry Shop Owners' Corporation, (not so affectionately referred to by the owners as the "sweat-sock.") Peeling paint was probably the last thing he'd have time to notice, but he and Mary would appreciate the information, she was sure of that.

She jogged on past Marla's Bakery and Cafe, dark and locked, and Flowers by Daisy — the florist shop — next door to that. She ran around the old metal dumpster parked at the corner of Daisy's shop: an ugly beast with a heavy lid that could kill a person, Po thought. The one down at Selma's end of the alley looked far more benign — perhaps she'd suggest they replace this eyesore.

Daisy's shop was surprisingly quiet. Po glanced at the locked door as she went by. Strange. Usually Daisy Sample, the owner, was here by now — one of the few signs of life Po would encounter on her Saturday run. Her battered pick-up would be parked beside the back door, and Daisy herself would be hoisting baskets filled with fresh flowers and plants from the back and carrying them into the shop. Rising at dawn most Saturdays, Daisy was first in line at the Kansas City market to make sure she got the best of the pickings. Daisy Sample was a puzzle, Po thought; she found the most beautiful plants and cut flowers in a one hundred-mile radius and brought them back to Crestwood to sell in her store; she arranged them in buckets and vases that rivaled arrangements Po had seen in hotels and at elegant events. But beyond the flowers, Daisy's shop was a lesson in bad taste, with rotting window boxes out front holding plastic flowers, and a clutter of objects that caused some of the shop owners to compare it to a miniature golf course. She had heard recently that Owen Hill and the two other directors of ESOC had come down hard on Daisy, telling her to shape up or face expulsion. In a rage, Daisy had thrown a pot of mums at Owen's car. An anger management course was definitely in order, Po thought. She looked around to see if Daisy's truck was parked further down the alley. It wasn't in sight, and Po decided that Daisy must have gotten a late start this morning, too.

Po glanced to her right, cautiously eyeing the still-shadowed walkway that separated Marla's and Daisy's from the rest of the block, and jogged on past Brew and Brie, the gourmet liquor, wine and cheese shop; August Schuette's Elderberry Bookstore, and an empty spot that she suspected would be rented soon. There was talk of an elegant small bistro. Elderberry Road was a choice location. Next was a small gallery and stationery shop that would be opening soon.

Po ran on, down toward the alley's end where dear Selma's shop anchored the block with its colorful fabrics and quilts. She scanned the back of the buildings as she jogged, a habit born of curiosity, and wondered how long Selma would keep the shop going. Business wasn't great and she'd talked on and off of closing this year, a thought that saddened everyone who knew her, and especially Po and the other Queen Bee quilters who spent nearly every Saturday — and some weeknights as well — in the delightful sanctuary of Selma's back room, working on some quilt project. The Queen Bees had designed and made baby quilts, small quilted wall hangings, and two quilts of Kansas flowers that were raffled for benefits. Sometimes they worked on their own projects, and other times they worked together, each making a special square that became a part of a whole, like the project they were planning now — an anniversary quilt in honor of the fiftieth anniversary of the quilt store. Selma Parker, and her mother before her, had owned Parker's Dry Goods for almost fifty years. And more neighborhood kids than Po could count —

including both of her own — had come home from the hospital wrapped in a flannel quilt that was created in Selma's back room.

A shrill cat cry pierced through her thoughts and Po slowed down slightly, her eyes searching for the source of the plaintive sound. She jogged back a few steps, then forward again, sucking in a lung-full of air as her pace slowed. She wiped the stream of perspiration from her forehead with the back of her hand, then bent low at the waist and peered into the bushes near the edge of the alley. "Here, kitty, kitty," she coaxed.

The cat answered almost immediately and Po spotted it then, not behind the bushes, but on the other side of the alley, sitting on the lid of a dumpster that was parked near the back of Selma's shop. The cat was coal-black — long and slender with a tail that batted the air in rhythmic, deliberate swoops. It stared intently at Po.

"Looking for food, sweetheart?" Po asked. She jogged in place in front of the cat, but the animal didn't move. "I'd head back to Marla's if I were you. I suspect you'll find much better pickings at her back door than you will here."

Seeming to heed Po's suggestion, the cat jumped off the dumpster. But instead of heading back down the alley, it ran directly to the back door of the quilt shop, pulling Po's gaze along with it.

And then, in an instant, Po saw it. What that lovely black cat had wanted her to see all along, she suspected, and confided as much to her friends later. The back door of Selma Parker's quilt shop, open — not all the way — but just enough for the cat to slip in and out. And holding it open, just as sure and steady as one of Daisy's stone garden statues, was the still body — or more precisely, the right foot — of dear Owen Hill, the best damn department chair Canterbury College had ever had.

◆

CHAPTER 2

Trail of Friendship

Kate Simpson had been back in Crestwood for 18 months — and a member of the Queen Bee quilters for nearly half that time. And in all those months, she had never been on time for a single Saturday quilting session. Today, unfortunately, would be no exception.

Kate ran down the back steps of her childhood home on Evergreen Street, slung a worn backpack over one shoulder, and jumped on her bike. "Mama Mia," she murmured as she pedaled down the drive, spewing gravel in all directions. A tangled mass of hair fanned out behind her — thick bronze and reddish brown streaks.

"You're late, little Katie," old Danny Halloran shouted. He was ambling up the long driveway next door, his fat Saturday *Kansas City Star* tucked firmly between his arm and a plaid bathrobe flapping open and shut against his knobby knees.

Nearly five foot eight in her stocking feet — and at least three inches taller than her elderly neighbor — Kate wasn't called *little* by many people. Danny could get away with it because he'd lived next door to the Simpsons since before Kate was born. "I'd be even later, Danny," she called back, "if those blasted sirens hadn't knocked me straight out of bed. What the heck is going on?" She knew that Danny was always up at dawn, and at the first sound of the sirens, he'd have headed straight for his police scanner.

"Don't know, little one. Doggone scanner wasn't working this morning — darn thing isn't worth a tinker's dam. But even with this confounded hearing aid — " he pointed with his free hand to his ear, "I sure heard 'em. Must be a fire over near the college. Or maybe one of those crazy fraternity parties tearing the town apart." He shook his round, bare head. "Damn crazy kids. What's the world coming to?"

"Hard to say, Danny," Kate said. "But I know you're heading for a case of pneumonia if you don't get on in that house. You'll catch your death of cold. Besides, you're indecent."

"Bossy as my Ella," he shot back to her. "Get on with you now. And let me know what all that racket's about, you hear?" He swatted the air with the rolled up newspaper and struggled up the steps to his door.

Kate waited to be sure he made it safely inside, then pedaled quickly down the quiet street and around the corner toward the Elderberry shops. She'd promised dear Po she'd at least try to be on time this week, though she suspected her godmother was happy enough if she just showed up.

The weekly meetings made it easier for Po to honor the request Kate's mom had made to Po before she died last year — "Keep an eye on Kate, Po ... keep her safe." That's probably what she'd said to her closest, life-long friend — that, or something to that effect. Kate knew that her mom had also told Po to encourage Kate to go back to Boston if she wanted to, back to the life she had abandoned in the blink of an eye when her mother got sick. "Send her back, then call her often," her mother would have said.

But for reasons that even Kate herself didn't completely understand, she'd decided not to go back to her cozy Brookline apartment after her mother died. "Not yet," she had told Po, "but soon" — whatever the heck that meant. And here she was, all these months later, still in Crestwood, still living in the three-bedroom house her mom had left her. And if that weren't enough to make her mom smile from her "new place," she was spending every Saturday morning at her mother's old quilting bee, of all the crazy things.

Joining the Queen Bees quilting group was not something Kate had planned. But Po had been pushy about it, and it was hard — no, make that impossible — to say no to that woman, even if you had two left thumbs and knew diddlysquat about quilting.

Kate had found most of the quilting supplies that she needed in a black trunk, pushed to the back of her mother's

11

closet after she got sick. Kate savored the time she spent going through the neat stacks of bright, lovely fabrics that her mother had separated by color and pattern and intensity — calico from stripes, mini from large prints. And beneath all her grumbling about joining the Queen Bees, Kate suspected that was exactly why Po had insisted she try her hand at quilting — because fingering the washed colorful fabrics and breathing in the smell of lilac that permeated everything her mother had touched, brought a bit of Meg Simpson right smack back into Kate's life.

The scream of a second siren broke into Kate's thoughts just as she turned onto Elderberry Road. She braked to a stop directly in front of Marla's Bakery and Café and watched the police car speed by. Its spinning light splashed red shadows across the front of Flowers by Daisy, the Elderberry Bookstore, and on down the block of uneven brick stores until it screeched to a stop — directly in front of Selma Parker's quilt shop.

Phoebe Mellon had been up for nearly two hours. Not by choice, lord knows, but neither God nor man could keep Jude and Emma, her eleventh-month-old twins, asleep past 6 o'clock. And then those blasted sirens scared little Emma half to death and Phoebe had her hands full with diapers and nursing and crying babies. Finally she settled them both in the playpen, diapered and happy with dribbles of mother's milk collecting in the corner of their mouths, and she shook her sleeping husband awake.

"It's Saturday, Jimmy dear," she said sweetly, planting a kiss on his forehead. "And I'm off to my quilting bee."

James Burgess Mellon III groaned. He pulled one eye open and watched his bride of not quite two years slip out of her robe and into a pair of jeans and tee shirt. Even in jeans, no make-up, and her hair a floppy mess of white-gold waves, Phoebe excited him. He'd fallen in love with all five feet of her the first night he laid eyes on her. He was standing alone at the bar at Nick's — a law student hangout — and there she was, bulldozing her way through that mass of inflated egos and legal brawn, a loaded platter of beers hoisted high above her head. And he'd fallen for her hook, line and sinker. They were married the day after his law school graduation, and barely nine months later, Jude and Emma burst into their small world and filled it to the brim.

"Well?" Phoebe said now, grinning down at him. Sunlight from the bedroom window lit her from behind and her hair frizzed up around her head like a halo. "Better get yourself out of that bed right now or I'll be tempted to do evil things."

"Hmmmmm," Jim murmured.

Phoebe pulled the covers up over his head. "Later, love. You need to earn your keep. Our beautiful babes are in the playpen. I'm outta here."

Phoebe blew him another kiss, spun around and headed toward the back door of the house that her in-laws had given them for a wedding present. Phoebe knew the Mellons didn't like her much, and the house was an attempt to disguise the fact that she had been a barmaid and pierced her ears far more than was socially acceptable at the Crestwood Country Club. The fact that she worked in a bar to pay her way through college because her family didn't have a dime, didn't seem to alter the Mellons' opinion. So they tried to make her more to their liking by wrapping her up in a lovely home and a membership to their club. "It's the 'My Fair Lady' approach," Phoebe explained to the Queen Bees in her best Eliza Dolittle imitation: 'I'll be a proper wife in a proper house, I will.' And then she'd giggled — that Goldie Hawn ripple that soon had them all pushing their quilting squares aside and reaching for tissues to dab the laughter from the corners of their eyes.

The house was nice, Phoebe admitted, although she still wasn't used to it — who needed three bathrooms? But the yard would be great for the kids, and Jim seemed to like the place, so she'd moved on in and even tried her best to keep it looking decent.

Phoebe checked the twins one final time, planting kisses on their sweet-smelling heads. What absolutely wondrous little people they are, she thought. Then she grabbed a jacket off the brass hook in the back hallway and flew out the door, bounding across the street and down the few short blocks to the Elderberry shops.

For the fourth time in as many days, Maggie Helmers couldn't get her truck started. A brief trip under the hood with pliers seemed to do the trick. "Soon, dear truck," she said out loud, patting the hood affectionately, "I may have to put you out to pasture."

A glance at her oversized wristwatch convinced her to let the grease smudges remain on her nose and cheeks until she got to Selma's. She climbed into the pickup and sped off across town toward the Elderberry shops.

It took fifteen minutes for Maggie to drive from her veterinary clinic at the edge of Crestwood to Elderberry Road. These Saturday mornings at Selma's were darn near sacred to her — she wouldn't miss them for anything, even though it didn't make practical sense to close her veterinary clinic for those three or four prime Saturday hours. Her ex-husband told her she was crazy to forgo that extra revenue, but Maggie had laughed at that. She figured that anyone who had lost thousands of dollars at Kansas City's gambling boats and then tried to sue them for encouraging the addiction didn't have much right to judge other people's sanity.

Quilting was her therapy, and Maggie savored every single minute of it — from picking the colors and choosing the fabrics, to cutting shapes and pinning it all together in a marvelous, intricate pattern. And she loved the circle of women whose company she shared every Saturday morning. The group was an odd hodgepodge who might not have found each other in ordinary life, but the quilting gathered them together, and they opened their lives to each other. They even shared Maggie's passion for "fat-lady"art, finding pieces to add to her collection at art fairs and small galleries.

Maggie had started her art collection for fun — a grand celebration of grande women. But with the help of friends and family, it was growing into an amazing collection that included a Mexican collage of old women praying at the sea, smooth voluptuous soapstone statues, and a lovely carving. The Queen Bees encouraged her, and rejoiced over each new find, and they always knew just what to get her for her birthday.

Having Kate come back to town was a special bonus in Maggie's life, too, even better than the collection of beautiful fat-lady art that filled her small home. Though Kate was a half-dozen years younger than she, Maggie had known her all her life. They'd grown up in the same neighborhood, practically sisters, and to have Kate stay on after Meg Simpson passed was a gift Maggie relished.

Maggie crossed the Emerald River separating the two sides of town, cut through a narrow one-way street that wound through the edge of Canterbury College (an illegal shortcut, but not patrolled on Saturdays), and spun around the corner onto Elderberry Road, her spare tire and toolbox sliding noisily across the flat bed of her truck. Ahead, toward the end of the block, she spotted a crowd of people, an unusual sight at this hour on a Saturday morning. Only Marla's opened this early, and the street was usually quiet. Not today. Maggie pulled over to the curb, jammed the gearshift into first, set the brake, and jumped out of the cab.

Canterbury College was small in size and big in reputation. The large stone buildings, complete with ivy-covered walls, were nearly picture perfect — a fact several Hollywood producers had discovered and used to their advantage in filming movies on location in Crestwood. Cheap, picturesque, and full of friendly people everywhere, that was the word that got out.

Leah Sarandon remembered seeing one of those movies back east and wondering where its lovely location was — Connecticut? New Hampshire? Kansas, of course, would not have entered her mind, yet here she was, all these years later, a tenured Canterbury professor, walking across a movie-set campus that had become a cherished home to her.

Leah picked up her pace and breathed in the crisp autumn

air. Her long denim skirt brushed lightly against her ankles. People thought of Kansas and imagined tornadoes — not autumn days that touched on sheer perfection — with gentle breezes shaking crimson leaves from their branches — or unimaginable spring weeks with a startling profusion of pink and white dogwoods, deep red crabapple trees — tulips and daffodils and pansies spilling from yards and flower boxes. Leah loved the raw energy that the seasons poured into her soul.

And she loved this Saturday morning quiet, too, the lovely lazy lull that allowed the whole campus to gear up for another week of learning. She had the small campus almost to herself, with just an occasional student or teacher headed toward the library for research or to the commons for coffee and maybe an early study session. She waved at a student, shifted her tote bag on her shoulder and headed toward the far corner of campus and a large fenced-in home that anchored the school on the west side.

Canterbury House, it was called, the place where Elliott Canterbury settled his family more than a century ago so he could build a thriving fur trading business along the banks of the Emerald River. (Local lore had it that whoever coined the name Emerald for this muddy river was thinking green for money.) Once done, he decided the town folks needed a college, and so he built them one in his backyard. It was separated from his large three-story home by a wrought iron fence and an iron-tight will that made sure the college could never force family out of Canterbury House, or worse, tear it down. As long as there were Canterburys that wanted to live in the house, the house would be theirs.

Trail of friendship

Leah's dear friend Eleanor was the sole current resident — the eighty-two-year-old great-granddaughter of the college founder. Leah spotted her ahead, her hand resting on a wrought iron fence finial, and quickened her pace.

"Hurry up, Leah," Eleanor yelled out. "You're poking along like an old lady." She followed up with a strong, soaring laugh that spun on the quiet air. Eleanor was as unpredictable as Kansas weather — and Leah never tired of her. The college students didn't know what to think of her, and rumors percolated each fall with the new crop of freshmen. Tales of ghosts and spirits seen late at night in Canterbury House windows punctuated cafeteria gossip — and Eleanor loved every minute of it.

"What's that racket, Leah?" she asked now, her clear blue eyes looking into the distance.

"Sounds like sirens to me," Leah said, picking up Eleanor's quilting bag and lifting it over her shoulder. "There's probably a cat stuck up in a tree somewhere."

Eleanor laughed again and took Leah's arm. In her other hand she gripped a carved walking stick that helped her along uneven sidewalks and foot paths. She also used it often in heated conversations. "A little excitement in paradise. But let's think big, Leah. Perhaps there's a dastardly deed been done on Elderberry Road. And if so, my dear, I most definitely don't want to miss out. Onward."

♦

C H A P T E R 3

Streak of Lightning

Kate looked down the street at the small crowd gathering on the corner across from Selma's shop. She spotted Phoebe immediately, her loose hair wild and lit by sunshine. She was standing on the edge of the crowd, staring at the quilt shop. "Phoebe," Kate called at the top of her voice and pedaled fast down the street toward her friend.

"What's all this?" Phoebe demanded to Kate.

Kate slid off her bike and propped it against the lamp post. "I don't know Pheebs. I heard sirens," she said. "And a police car nearly ran me off the road."

The two young women stared across the street, shielding their eyes from the sun and trying to see through the plate glass windows. The crowd began to spill over into the street and in minutes, the others were there — Leah, Eleanor, and Maggie — all hovering around the lamppost like moths. "I tried to park my truck where I always do on Saturdays — in the alley behind the store," Maggie said. She was slightly out of breath. "But I couldn't get through — there's an ambulance back there — right outside Selma's back door."

"Is Selma all right?" Leah asked.

"I haven't seen her — they won't let anyone in," Phoebe said.

"Where's Po?" Kate pushed her sunglasses into her mass of auburn hair and stared across the street. She wrapped her arms tightly around her chest, squeezing back the fear.

"There she is!" Phoebe pointed across the street. And with great relief, the covey of quilters strained to see through the shop window. Several uniformed men and women scurried back and forth in front of bright bolts of fabric. And there in the center of it all was Selma Parker, a calm solid figure in the middle of the tempest, Po at her side. Eleanor squinted through her thick prescription sunglasses. "They both look fine."

"Susan!" Phoebe yelped, anxious to account for each Queen Bee. "Can anyone see her in there? I can't see with all the police in the way."

Susan Miller had been a godsend to Selma, hiring on as assistant manager of the store the year before and allowing Selma to take an occasional day off, here and there. The

Queen Bees had promptly adopted her, pulling her into the group to fill a space left by Helga Hansen, who had moved to Omaha. Susan's artistic eye, her innate sense of color and her flair for pushing a piece of traditional into a patch of extraordinary had urged the Bees on to new and adventurous ways of quilting. They still loved their traditional patchwork projects, but often, under Susan's guidance, they played with new ideas — transforming photographs into quilt patterns, combining appliqué, patchwork, and needlework into single projects. Susan kept things fresh and exciting.

"Susan's okay. I see her, but she looks a little distraught." Kate pointed to the west side of the store where a slender figure was bent over in a straight back chair, her head in her hands.

At that moment, Po emerged from the store and scanned the crowd. She spotted the Queen Bees and quickly crossed the street.

"I have sad news," she said quietly, before anyone had a chance to speak or to ask her what was going on inside.

Kate's heart rose to her throat. Phoebe's eyes grew larger. Leah stared at her friend. "Out with it, Po," Eleanor commanded.

"Owen Hill has died."

Kate stared at Po. "What do you mean, died? That's impossible. I just saw him yesterday afternoon on campus."

"Well, he wasn't dead then, Kate," Po said. "But he is now."

Leah blanched. She had known Owen Hill since coming to Canterbury College as a young professor fifteen years before. He had been a mentor and friend. "I can't believe this," she said. "What happened, Po?"

"We don't know yet. Heart attack, maybe. It looks like he fell hard and hit his head. They've just now taken him away."

"When did it happen?" Phoebe stuck her hands into the pockets of her jeans and lifted herself onto the toes of her tennis shoes, straining to see any new developments across the street. "Po, this is so awful! Poor Selma — a man dying in her store."

Maggie edged in between Kate and Phoebe. "Is Selma all right, Po?"

"She'll be okay," Po said. "She has her hands full right now. The police answer those emergency calls as well as the ambulance, so there are plenty of folks crawling around inside our quilt store."

Leah's oval face was pale and her clear brown eyes registered distress. "Owen and I were on a committee together this semester. I saw him nearly every day on campus. You don't think about people like Owen Hill dying."

"Why was he at Selma's?" Eleanor asked.

Eleanor's practical question released a stream of others:

"Is Susan okay?"

"Where was Mary?"

"Where did he die?"

"What can we do?"

Questions flew like quilting needles, drowning Po's voice. Finally she shushed the Queen Bees with a fanning of her hands. "I think there actually is something we can do. We can gather our quilting equipment, head to my house, and get to work planning this anniversary quilt for Selma," she said. "That's what we can do."

The Paltrow home, where Po had lived for over thirty years, was everyone's favorite place "to stop and flop," as, Kate put it. The rambling white frame house, surrounded by a sixteen-foot-wide porch, was just a short mile from the Elderberry shops. It was in the heart of a gracious old neighborhood, filled with comfortable homes, giant elm trees and old maples that turned the yards into fiery paintings each fall. Many professors from nearby Canterbury College had raised their families in the closely-knit neighborhood. Po and Sam had raised their own children there, but often said it was the village of which Hillary Clinton spoke — and Sam had joked that it had taken every single one of those villagers to help them raise their three.

Phoebe, Kate, and Maggie squeezed together in Maggie's truck, with Kate's bike rattling around in the back, and were the first to reach Po's. Turning into the drive, they cruised past the bordering crabapple hedges and pulled to a stop in front of the three-car garage.

"I love this house," Kate murmured, looking up at the battered basketball hoop, the scene of many late-night games of H.O.R.S.E.

"Me, too," Maggie said. She tossed her keys into an enormous leather purse and followed Kate and Phoebe around to the back door. "It's the kind of house that looks at you, opens its arms and says, 'Hey, you, whoever you are — come on in. Be safe. Be comfortable. Be happy,"

Kate smiled. Safe. Comfortable. Happy. She had been all of those things in this house. Her mother and Po never went more than a day or two without getting together, and when she was little, Kate was always in tow.

"I think the first time I ever met you was right here on this lawn," Kate said to Maggie. "You were with Po's daughter, Sophie."

"And Po told Sophie and me that we had to watch her best friend's little girl while they talked girl-talk in the sunroom. So there we were, stuck with this scrawny, gangly little kid," she snorted, "with orders to treat little Katie Simpson like a gentle lamb."

"Gentle lamb, my foot," Kate laughed. "And I was never scrawny, Maggie. You know that."

"Oh, shush, you're gorgeous. Always were. Disgusting but true."

"And what did you do, Mags? Ditch her?" Phoebe asked. "That's what my brothers always did with me."

"Nope. Kate was ornery enough that we couldn't get away with that. But we did send her in to ask for Cokes and cookies because Po spoiled her rotten."

Phoebe laughed and Kate pushed open the door. Like many of the neighbors, Po never locked her doors, a fact Kate took for granted growing up. But now, after living in Boston for a few years, it made her cringe.

Maggie and Phoebe followed her into the sunny kitchen and family room combination that stretched across the entire back of the house. Hoover, Po's contented Irish Setter, was sprawled across the couch.

"Hoover," Kate called over to him. "Shame on you."

Hoover's tail flopped joyfully on the pillows, inviting gentle ear scratching and accepting no blame for his indiscretion. Maggie walked over, sat down on the edge of the sofa, and happily complied.

The sunny room was filled with years of memories for Kate. Beyond the wall of windows was the wide back porch, cluttered with comfortable wicker chairs and porch swings, huge wooden paddle fans, and a lush, rolling backyard that had once been a woods. When the house was built, Po and Sam had insisted that as many trees be kept as possible, and it was filled with river oak, fifty-foot pine trees, and a thick, brambly blackberry patch that yielded the fruit for Po's famous berry cobblers.

"This place was our playground," Kate said, looking across the yard, then around the well-stocked kitchen. At the far end of the open area was a floor-to-ceiling stone fireplace and soft comfortable couches with a table between. Sam Paltrow had made the coffee table himself — an enormous square chunk of oak, worn to a shine over the years and host to many a Scrabble game. Overstuffed chairs were grouped in a pair near a thick bookcase on another wall, and a third sat close to the wide French doors that led out to the porch.

After years of hide-and-seek on all floors of the Paltrow home, Kate was as familiar with it as her own. She loved the wide polished hallways and the cozy den at the front of the house. It was paneled in thick walnut with built-in book-shelves that climbed all the way to the ceiling, and to this day, it still smelled of Sam's Swisher Sweets cherry-scented cigars. There, while adults clinked glasses and chatted in front of the fireplace or out on the porch, a small body could make its way easily into the cabinets below the bookcases. And wedged in between stacks of musty-smelling National Geographics, poker chips, and jigsaw puzzles, Kate would shush herself into quiet while the older kids ran through the house looking for her. She loved it here.

While Kate rummaged around in the refrigerator looking for Po's coffee beans, Phoebe pulled her cell phone out of her backpack and called home, checking on Jude, Emma, and Jimmy. Kate had long suspected that as much as Phoebe savored her Saturday mornings with the Queen Bees, it wouldn't be quite so lovely if her three loves, as she called them, weren't connected to her frequently used cell phone.

"News travels fast," said Phoebe, snapping down the lid of her phone and slipping it into the pocket of her jeans. "Jimmy said three neighbors and a lawyer from his firm had already called to see if we'd heard the news about Owen's death. Peter Finch — he lives next door — said that Selma had a lot of things going on in that back room, drugs maybe! And maybe that's why Owen Hill had a heart attack."

Just then, Leah and Eleanor arrived, balancing white bakery boxes and satchels of quilting materials. "Phoebe!" Leah scolded. "What trash."

"Of course it is," Phoebe said. She walked over and flopped down on one of the wide corduroy-covered couches. Her tiny body was nearly lost in its cushions. "It's preposterous, is what it is, and that's exactly what Jimmy told Peter. He also told him a little about slander suits and said that he was offering Selma a special on them if she was interested."

"That's our Jimmy." Leah smiled and began taking blueberry muffins and Marla's cinnamon rolls out of one of the boxes, placing them on a large platter. Maggie straddled a chair at the thick dining table and picked at the stray crumbs that fell onto the tabletop.

Kate waited for the comforting gurgle of the coffeemaker,

then sat down opposite Phoebe and unzipped her backpack. "I'd almost forgotten how much people gossip in this town."

"People gossip, sure," Leah said. "But people also care. Sometimes that's at the root of it."

"But to imply that drugs were involved because a lovely man dies of a heart attack? That's just crazy. I love this little town, but that kind of thing reminds me of when I was a kid and my parents knew before I got home at night, whose car I'd been riding in," Kate said. "Or if I'd sneaked a cigarette with a friend down by the river — nothing was secret."

"There's that side of it. But I still think it usually comes down to concern, at least more often than not. I've lived on both coasts and had great friends there, but I love the caring of near-strangers here." Leah finished arranging the muffins and sat down on the couch next to Eleanor.

"Not to perpetuate the gossip, you understand," Phoebe said, "but what was Owen doing at Selma's, anyway?" She began pulling small pieces of fabric from her quilting sack and lining them up on the large coffee table between her and Kate.

"Po said there'd been a meeting of that corporation the shop owners formed," Leah said. "All the shop owners were there — we'll have to wait for her to tell us more."

"Where is she, anyway?" Kate asked.

"Selma and Susan called her back over to the store just as we were getting ready to leave. She told us to go on without her and she'd be here soon. She'd catch a ride with someone," she said. Leah sat at the large trestle table, lifted her square, hand-made quilting case onto the table, and unsnapped the strap that held it together.

"I took an art history class from Dr. Hill last semester," Kate said. "And his lectures on 'Art of the Ages' were always standing-room only. He brought art history to life." She looked over at Maggie. "Maggie, you took care of the Hill's dog, didn't you?" Kate asked.

Maggie nodded. "They had an amazing golden named Spencer. He was a beautiful, wonderful dog. But it was usually Mary Hill, who came in with Spencer." Maggie poured a cup of coffee, remembering. "Oh, except once," she said. "It was Professor Hill who brought Spencer in the day we had to put him to sleep. He was old — his back legs had given out and he just couldn't get up anymore. I remember how kind Owen Hill was, holding that big golden bundle in his arms the whole time, stroking his fur and whispering sweet words into his ear. He said Mary just couldn't do it."

They looked up and listened as a car pulled into the drive, followed by a door slam, and the car rolling out again. In seconds, Po breezed through the door. "Hi, everyone," she said, walking quickly across the kitchen and pouring a cup of coffee. Hoover leapt off the couch and hurried to her side. "I'm glad you're all here."

Kate was threading a needle for Eleanor so she could sew the ribbing on a pillow she was almost finished with. The long piece of cobalt-blue thread dangled from her fingers. She looked up over the needle and met Po's eyes. Po was standing still at the kitchen counter, and the face that Kate considered one of the loveliest in her life was pinched in worry.

"Po?" she said. "Are you okay?"

At that, the others looked up, too.

Po walked toward them, her eyes glancing out the back

windows into the blanket of fall color. Finally she looked back at her circle of friends. They were all looking at her expectantly.

"Po, you're white as a ghost," Kate said. "Please sit down." She started to rise from the couch.

Po stopped her with an outstretched hand. "I'm fine, honey. But I have some bad news, as if we haven't heard enough today. Owen Hill didn't die of a heart attack."

"An aneurysm, I bet," Phoebe said. "Jimmy's Uncle Frederick had one burst right in the middle of a speech at the Kiwanis Club . . ."

A gentle shake of Eleanor's head shushed Phoebe. The only sound in the room was the nervous tap of Eleanor's cane against the hardwood floor.

"Owen Hill was murdered," Po said.

◆

C H A P T E R   4

H e a r t s   &   H a n d s

"Murdered!" Five voices collided in mid-air.

Po sat down on a chair beside Maggie. "I was jogging behind the alley when I first saw Owen lying there in the doorway. He had blood on the back of his head . . ." Po paused and squeezed her eyes shut for a minute. The image of Owen Hill was startlingly clear, a brutal snapshot imprinted across the front of her brain. Would it ever go away? She took a deep breath and began again. "But we thought — I thought — that it was because he fell and hit his head."

"And?" coaxed Phoebe. She was sitting on the edge of her chair.

"This is awful, Po," Leah murmured.

"No, this is impossible," Phoebe broke in. Her blonde head shook with the force of her words. "People kill each other in Boston . . ." she looked over at Kate as if she were personally responsible for that fact. "Not here in Crestwood. That's why Jimmy and I stayed here. That's why we're having our babies here."

"Honey — ," Eleanor said, leaning forward in her chair and tapping Phoebe's thigh with her cane, "unfortunately people can kill people anywhere they want. But this is still among the better places to have your babies, I suspect."

"Was it a burglar?" Maggie asked. She'd been concerned about break-ins at her veterinary clinic and had installed extra locks and alarms to make sure the pharmaceuticals were safe. Selma's shop didn't have drugs, for sure, but you never knew what people were looking for.

"It might have been a burglar," Po said. "They don't know much yet."

Kate hadn't said a word. She watched Po, her mind spinning. A heart attack was one thing — that sometimes happens to people and it's sad and of course you miss the person terribly. But murder! Phoebe was right this time — murders happened in Boston — lots of them. And in New York. Even in Kansas City. But not in Crestwood, Kansas.

"Why would anyone break into Selma's shop," Maggie asked.

"Good question, Maggie," Phoebe said. "Good grief —

what would they expect to find there — is there a black market on quilts?"

"Why not break into the fancy wine store down the block?" Leah said. "Or Mary and Owen's own antique store? It would have more valuables and more money than Selma's."

"Maybe the burglar had the wrong store," Phoebe suggested. "I'll bet it's hard to see in that alley at night."

Speculations were tossed out into the middle of the room as each woman fumbled around for the right patches of fabric in her bag, opened containers of straight pins and set them on Po's wide oak table or the coffee table in front of the couch. It was finish-up-Saturday, as Phoebe called it. They were each finishing up their individual quilts or hangings or place mats so they could begin work in earnest on an anniversary quilt for Selma.

Phoebe went into the laundry room and came back with an ironing board and iron. She plugged it in, waiting to feel heat against her fingers. "The most peculiar thing about this whole business is that Owen was there alone. What was he doing there, Po?"

"Selma said they had had a shop owner's meeting last night. They were trying to get some things worked out and settle some arguments."

"What kind of arguments?" Phoebe began ironing the seams of the squares that made up a Thanksgiving table runner, pressing them away from the stitching, as Selma had taught her. She looked up from the ironing board.

"Just normal business things. For one, they were trying to get Daisy to spruce up her place. Selma said Daisy left in a fury, outraged at Owen for being told what to do with her shop. And they were discussing replacing the sidewalk, things like that. Owen had indicated they'd have to meet again soon. He wanted to call some audits, make sure all the contractors were legal, that sort of thing."

"Sounds boring," Phoebe said.

"It is." Maggie rolled her eyes. "I love owning my own clinic, but the paperwork is horrendous. And I don't have to bother with other owners the way those folks do."

"Why did Owen stay later than the others?" Eleanor asked.

"He and Max Elliott — he's both lawyer and accountant for that group — stayed for a short while to figure out some problems with a lease for that new stationery store. Then Max left, and Owen stayed on to wrap things up. Max said it wasn't unusual for him to do that. Selma gave him a key a long time ago since they met so often in her store and some-times she didn't come." Po poured herself another cup of coffee and then walked around the room, refilling everyone's cups.

"Well, what can we do?" Leah asked. "I suppose casseroles for Mary." Her long narrow fingers stitched the binding in place for a small pillow she was making for her grandmother. Her fingers moved rhythmically, with quiet assurance.

"That's a good idea," Po said, "though Mary was very active in her church. They might be taking care of that. I'll find out." She walked over to a closet and took out a box holding the pieces of fabric she was using to make a quilted wall hanging for her daughter Sophie's birthday. She'd taken photographs of Sophie and her baby, Jane, and transferred them to pieces of fabric. Susan and Leah had ingeniously come up with a quilting pattern that circled the photos and tied them into a wondrous whole. All that was left was the binding, which she was ready to stitch in place. It was a good day to work on something for loved ones, she decided — it shrunk the distance between Sophie's home in Oregon and hers in Crestwood — and dimmed the morning's horror.

"Do you think Selma will be okay?" Kate asked. "Is Susan with her?"

Po nodded. "I don't know which of them is more shaken by this, Susan or Selma. Susan came in early this morning, so she was there when the police were photographing Owen's body. Needless to say, it was difficult for her."

"Poor Susan. Sometimes she seems so vulnerable. I have a class with her this semester and she's so quiet, but when she speaks, it's always worth listening to." Kate stood and headed for the kitchen table.

"But she's solid and strong when she needs to be, I suspect," Po said. "I've seen her with some of Selma's more difficult customers."

"And you, Po?" Kate said. "How are you doing with all this?" Kate helped herself to a cinnamon roll, then walked over to Po. Maggie began folding up the ironing board while the others picked up frayed bits of fabric from the floor and began tying off threads. Kate watched Po carefully.

How was she? Po mulled the question around in her head. A friend was dead. Another in great distress over what had happened in her store. But the worst part of all was something Sam used to tease her about — that sixth sense, that kind of intuition that he said he could see in the pinch of her brow and set of her chin. And she felt it today. It settled over

35

Hearts & Hands

her like a heavy shroud — a deep, unsettling foreboding that this was only the beginning of their troubles. She looked up at Kate, standing still beside her.

"All's well that ends well, my Kate — let's hope that's what happens here." But she didn't for a minute believe a good end would come soon — and she knew that Kate didn't believe it either.

CHAPTER 5

Twisted Ribbons

Three days later, Po, Kate, and Maggie rode together to the Hill home. The three-story Tudor home stood at the crest of a hill, not far from Canterbury College. It looked over the whole town.

"Nice place," Maggie said, understating the elegance spread out before them.

"A good match for the funeral," Kate said. "That was quite an elaborate service."

"Owen and Mary have been very generous to that church," Po said. Personally, she had thought the service a bit extravagant, not entirely to her taste. The altar flowers were so abundant that a steady chorus of sneezing accompanied the Reverend Gottrey's long-winded eulogy. But each to his own, she thought. She certainly wouldn't begrudge Mary Hill anything that might ease her grief.

Kate maneuvered her Jeep into a tight space near the end of the long driveway. "The Reverend was certainly appreciative of the Hills. In fact, his invitation to come back to the house to pay our respects sounded a bit like an order."

"I thought so, too," Maggie said. The dozens of cars packing the Hill circle drive indicated others had interpreted it the same way.

Owen Hill, Po reminded Kate, was almost solely responsible for Reverend Gottrey's new roof.

"A good turnout, in Reverend Gottrey's view, would be a good thing," Po said.

"Yes, but for whom?" Kate asked as she squeezed between two shiny SUVs and trudged up the hill. "Mary Hill can't be in much of a mood to entertain."

"She's the consummate hostess," Po said. "She'll hide her grief, greet us all graciously, and deal with Owen's death in the days to come."

Po looked back toward the street and noticed a policeman directing traffic. The quiet neighborhood of elegant homes had turned into a parking nightmare. She wondered how many of those making their way up the long walkway to Mary Hill's door were curiosity seekers. The drama of Owen Hill's death had taken over the town. It was talked about everywhere — from Dillon's Supermarket to the new Starbucks out near the mall — and the Canterbury College gossip mill was running at full steam. Even an editor at the small publishing house in Kansas City that was publishing Po's book on women and quilting called, asking all sorts of questions.

"Look — Phoebe and Leah beat us," Kate said as they walked through the front door and into a foyer that was far larger than Kate's living room. Phoebe and Leah stood beside a marble-topped table that held a silver urn of peach-colored roses. "Welcome to our cottage," Leah whispered.

"I've always wanted to come inside this house," Phoebe said, her face bright. A rosy-colored, wispy dress covered her small frame and several sets of gold earrings dangled from her ears. "Not like I wanted anyone to die to get me in, sure, but gads, just look at this place!"

"Quite nice for a professor," Kate admitted.

"Family money," sniffed a woman passing by.

Po looked after her, amused. "No secrets in this town," she said.

"I knew the Hills were wealthy, but I guess I never thought much about where it came from," Maggie said.

"Owen's father began a successful chain of hardware stores in Kansas City," Po said. "Owen wasn't interested in the business — art and teaching were his passions — so he sold everything when his father died, except the family farm. He was left with enough money to buy a small country."

"And he settled for the life of a professor in Crestwood," Kate said.

"He loved this town — and he loved teaching," Po said,

guiding the group toward the back of the house to make room for new guests. "Owen's farm is an amazing place, and he loved it with a special passion. It's not far from here, actually." She smiled to herself. "He called it a farm, but instead of cows and pigs, there are horses, acres of thick woods to hike in, and miles of rolling land that are perfect for cross-country skiing."

"How did he meet Mary?" Kate asked, following Po into a small vacant space beneath the winding staircase.

"They met in Kansas City, but they've lived here forever."

"Well, Mary Hill has done quite nicely for herself, that much is for sure," Phoebe whispered. "Just look at this place. And can you believe the size of that funeral? Makes me wonder who would come if I died. It would be so awful to have an empty church."

"I'll come, Pheebs," Kate assured her.

"Me, too," Maggie said. "I could bring a date. That'd be three."

"Thanks, guys. I know you'll never let me down." Her bubbly laughter caused several people to look at the group. Phoebe, as diminutive as an adolescent girl, still stood out in a crowd. Kate thought it was her amazing head of hair. Floozy hair, Phoebe's in-laws called it. Angel hair, the Queen Bees said.

Or it could have been the five tiny holes that dotted each ear. Phoebe explained to the Queen Bees once that each one represented a special memory — like her graduation, her wedding, the twins' birth. Eleanor had wondered aloud how many children Phoebe planned on having.

The tap of a cane on the highly polished floor announced Eleanor's approach. "Have you seen Mary yet?" she asked.

They shook their heads.

"I think she's out on the patio." Leah nodded toward open French doors at the back of the foyer. "It's probably much easier to breathe out there. I swear the entire town is here."

"I think the Reverend Gottrey imported people," Maggie said. "Surely there aren't this many people in all of Crestwood."

Leah laughed. "That man doesn't miss a trick, does he? Passing out memorial pledge envelopes for the Owen Hill memorial something or other before the ground has even closed over his casket."

"He was cremated," Phoebe said.

"Now, Phoebe — how do you know that?" Leah asked.

Phoebe looked around, then said in a whisper, "Well, he was. Janelle at Pierre's Salon told me. Mary Hill gets her hair done there, too. And Mary picked one of the grandest urns that Windsor House Antiques had to keep him in until she can take him — wherever it is you take urns with people in them. I think he's over there —" She inclined her head toward the open doors to a museum-like living room. A giant urn stood on the stone mantelpiece.

"Oh, Phoebe," Leah said, holding back a smile.

"There's Reverend Gottrey now," Po said, nodding toward the hallway.

The white-haired minister and his wife walked through the entryway, shaking every hand and thanking each person for coming. Po could hear him praising Owen Hill's grand contributions to God's work.

Leah frowned. "It doesn't seem to matter to the Reverend that Owen spent Sunday mornings on the golf course instead of at services."

"Mary came, though," Po said. "Religiously."

"And Professor Hill's money came, too," Phoebe said.

"And now there's this new memorial?" Maggie said. "Not bad."

"If he had to die, it's not a bad thing that someone benefits from it," Leah said resolutely. "I'm just sad, I guess. I liked Owen Hill so much, and it seems too soon to be talking about building memorials and coming up with ways to benefit from his death."

Po nodded. "Things seem more sinister when you're missing someone," she said.

"Or when that someone you're missing was murdered," Leah said sadly.

"I say we try to find Mary, shall we?" Kate made a move toward the French patio doors.

The group followed her out to the wide stone patio that wrapped around the back of Mary Hill's home. In the distance was a large swimming pool, covered for the season with a thick canvas tarp. Small pools of water weighed the canvas down here and there, and leaves stripped from the huge elms and maples along the side yard floated on the muddy, grim surface.

A maid stood at the door with a tray holding silver cups of spiced apple cider. Other staff moved about the quiet crowd, carrying trays of stuffed mushrooms and carpaccio on tiny toast points, mini cheese quiches, martinis and Manhattans. A small wine bar was set up near a fan of wide steps that led down to the swimming pool. "This is definitely like the most elegant funeral I've ever been too," Phoebe whispered. "It's more like a garden party." She looked around, then pointed toward the far end of the patio. "There's Mary Hill — "

Mary stood like a painting, flanked on either side by an ornate, potted fern. She was nearly still — a fragile, beautiful statue — greeting each guest with a slight, careful smile and a gentle lift of her brows, as if to apologize for bringing them to such a sad event. Her slate-black hair was wound tightly into a braided knot at the nape of her neck and her elegant silk suit fit her slender form perfectly.

She looked regal, Kate thought. And so familiar, standing there in her beautiful black suit. Then her eyes lit up with a memory pulled from her past. "Halloween," she said.

"Yes!" Maggie said. "I remember!"

"This was the 'don't miss' house," Kate explained to the others.

"I'd almost forgotten that," Po said. "You came back with marvelous things, not the small Hershey kisses and candied apples your mother and I handed out."

Kate laughed. "You and mom were definitely out of Mary's league, Po. The Hills gave us hand-dipped chocolates, Royals pennants, those wild troll dolls with the neon hair — very cool things," Kate said. "And remember, Mags, how Mary Hill used to dress up like a beautiful witch, dressed completely in black?"

"We thought she was the most amazing creature we had ever seen."

"She's definitely beautiful," Leah said. "It's funny, though — as many times as I've been in her company at university functions, I don't feel I know Mary at all. Owen seemed to do all the talking. She was an elegant appendage."

"I think that's because the university was Owen's turf," Po said. "But at church events — and the garden club and charity balls — Mary shined at those."

Po looked over and watched the circle of guests moving around Mary Hill. It was that sad, peculiar dance people did at wakes, and Po felt a sudden surge of empathy for the woman in the middle of it all.

Mary Hill looked up and saw Po watching her. Before Po could avert her eyes, Mary smiled at her. Then she excused herself from the group standing around her and walked across the patio to where the Queen Bees gathered.

"It was good of you all to come," Mary said, looking at each of them in turn. "The Queen Bees. But where's Selma?"

Just then Selma Parker walked over from the other direction. "Present and accounted for," she said, joining the group.

"I'm so glad you're here," Mary said

Selma frowned. "Well, now, where else would I be?"

Mary Hill slipped her arm through Selma's and drew her close to her side. The contrast between the two women — the tall, dark, elegant widow, and the round, flush-cheeked quilter with her thinning red hair slightly askew — would have been comical in any other setting.

"Will you be all right?" Mary asked Selma.

Selma straightened up in her unfamiliar heels. She looked intently at Mary. "Of course I'll be all right. Why wouldn't I be? I am not the one in need of concern."

"But it was your store —"

Po felt Selma tense.

"My store will be fine, Mary. I'll be fine, too." Selma seemed uncomfortable with Mary's arm in hers, but she didn't move away. "This whole damn thing is awful, but the only real sorrow is your pain, Mary. That's how I see it.

That's all."

Mary smiled gratefully. "And the others?"

For a minute Po thought Mary meant them, the Queen Bees, but when she followed the nod of Mary's head, she saw that she was looking at a small group of men and women standing near the wine bar on the edge of the patio. August Schuette from the bookstore stood with his back to them talking intently with Ambrose Sweet, co-owner with Jesse Farley of the Elderberry Road Brew and Brie. Daisy Sample and Max Elliott, the lawyer for the ESOC, were listening to the exchange.

Selma looked at them, then back at Mary. "We may have our disagreements — the whole silly bunch of us — but when push comes to shove, we'll never let one another down. Good grief, you know that, Mary. And Owen knew that, too. Sure, he made me mad sometimes, and others, too. But that means nothing. They'll all be here for you. And for me, for any of us. No matter what."

Po watched Mary's long fingers pinch and release the fabric of her black jacket.

"Thank you, Selma," Mary said finally. She smiled politely at the others in the group, then excused herself, and walked across the patio toward a new group of mourners waiting for her near the potted ferns. Kate noticed that she skirted the huddled storeowners and moved instead to a collection of university professors who stood near the patio steps.

"Now what was that all about?" Phoebe asked, straining her neck to see where Mary was going.

"Much ado about nothing," Selma said. "Owen was a director of the corporation that we formed when we bought the land on Elderberry Road. There were some disagreements recently, but they all pale in the light of Mary's loss. This isn't the place nor the time to talk about such things."

"Well, if looks could kill, we'd have another dead body, right here on this patio," Phoebe said. She nodded toward the group of shop owners.

August and Daisy were staring at Mary as she walked across the patio. Gus's glasses had slipped to the bulge near the end of his short fat nose and his thick brows were knit together in fierce concentration.

Selma shrugged. "Gus Schuette is a teddy bear with an awful face, that's all. I can't imagine what the good Lord had in mind in piecing that face together the way He did, but it's no fault of Gus's. Don't pay any attention to him. They're upset because as quiet as Mary is, she's no pushover. She's stubborn as a mule when it comes to getting what's best for her store."

"So why do the others care?" Phoebe asked. "I'd fight anyone tooth and nail to get what's best for my babies."

Po held back a smile. She had a fleeting image of the staid Crestwood PTA once Phoebe Mellon joined their group. They wouldn't know what hit them. "Mary's been pushing for a whole new advertising campaign. She thinks it would be good to advertise in *The New York Times.*"

"Why would she do that?" Leah asked.

"She thinks it will bring her the right kind of clientele. But she wants the corporation maintenance funds to pay for it. So that means we'd all be paying for it. Can't you see me luring folks from New York to my little quilt shop?" Selma shook her head. She laughed.

"Did Owen want to do that?" Maggie asked.

Selma shook her head. "Owen was sensible about it all. He was supporting the crazy brick sidewalk campaign that Mary and Ambrose started — but he knew it was foolish to advertise our little street back east."

Po watched as Gus turned back into his small group. The four shop owners looked like a mismatched sports team, huddled together on the football field. She and Gus were friends, and she knew all the others, too. They were all decent people, and just like everyone, they had their quirks and different views.

"I like Gus Schuette," Maggie said. "I always have. He never chased Kate and me out of his store, even when we ate chocolate covered peanuts in the kid's room, while reading the latest Judy Blume book. His bookstore was our favorite library."

"I still use it that way," Kate said. "I've written three papers curled up in one of those leather chairs."

"He's a decent man." Selma turned her back to the store-owners and took a glass of wine from a passing maid. Leah pointed out a mutual friend from the civic council and the two wandered off to say hello.

Phoebe excused herself to use the bathroom, but Maggie and Kate both knew she had gone to snoop around the elaborate home. That meant she'd be gone quite awhile.

Po spotted some empty chairs shielded from the rest of the patio by several small, carefully trimmed and potted bushes. "Does anyone else's feet hurt as much as mine?" she asked.

"Hurt? Mine are numb," Maggie said. She and Kate followed Po over to the chairs. Maggie promptly kicked off both black heels and shoved them beneath the chair with her big toe. "Let me tell you right now, dear friends, none of this dress-up stuff for my wake. It's jeans, pets, and country music — and if you don't obey, I will come back and haunt you for the rest of your lives."

"It's a plan."

Maggie stopped a passing maid and they each took a glass of wine from the silver tray.

Kate stretched her long legs in front of her and sighed. "Poor Mary Hill. Poor Selma. What a mess this is. I hope they find the murderer soon so things can get back to normal."

"I agree. But the police don't seem to have a clue. Julie Ames came in the clinic yesterday with Gwendolyn — her overweight basset. Julie works at the police station and she said it was probably a burglary, and they aren't exactly over-whelmed with clues."

"It just doesn't make sense, Maggie." Kate took a sip of her wine. "Even Selma says no self-respecting crook would come knocking — ."

"There's Susan," Maggie interrupted, pointing to a slender, pale woman standing near the door.

Po looked over. Susan Miller was ordinarily a very attrac-tive woman. Today she was three sheets to the wind. And it was clear that she wanted to be anywhere but where she was at that moment. Po waved until Susan spotted them. She hurried across the patio to join them.

"Here, Suze — this chair's for you." Kate pointed to a small chair tucked behind the urn.

"Thanks. You are lifesavers. I was about to turn around and leave. I only came because Selma asked me to. She thought since Mary's store is a part of the Elderberry group, that I should make an appearance." Susan's soft voice dropped off, and she reached into her jacket for a tissue.

Po handed her a glass of wine. "Here, Susan, have some wine. This may take the edge off. These gatherings are difficult."

Susan took a sip and managed a small smile in return. "It's just that this seems so inappropriate." She motioned toward the crowd. "All this lavishness, it's almost a celebration."

"Maybe it's just a different way to honor him, Susan," Maggie said. "People really loved him."

Susan looked at Maggie intently. "Did they?"

"Well, I think so, sure," Maggie said. She looked at Kate and Po for help.

"Well, maybe not everyone, but a lot of people," Kate said. "You went to that women's history lecture series he and Leah participated in last semester, Susan. You saw how everyone flocked to his talks. It was always packed to the rafters for his sessions. Owen and Leah were the draws, that's for sure."

"Maybe," Susan said. But her voice choked. "This is such a terrible thing. For Selma. For her shop. We're not doing very well anyway, and now this."

"But she has all of us to help her through it," Kate said. "And especially you, Susan. I know she leans on you a lot."

Susan took a sip of her wine and looked off into the crowd of mourners. She seemed to have forgotten the others were there. "Well, I'd do anything for Selma," she murmured. "Anything."

Kate and Po looked at each other.

"Sure you would," Maggie said.

Susan managed a wobbly smile and stood up. Then she lifted her wineglass and drank it down in one long swallow. "Would you all understand if I left? Please tell Selma that I was here. But I think I should go back to the store. I'm needed there more than I am here." She looked at Mary Hill standing across the patio, searched the crowd unsuccessfully for Selma, and then picked up her purse and hurried back into the house.

"Poor Susan — she certainly didn't want to be here," Maggie said, watching Susan hurry off.

"I guess we all react to stress in different ways," Po said.

"Yes. Take that group for example," Kate inclined her head toward the wine bar where some of the Elderberry shop owners were still gathered. Gus Schuette was frowning at something Daisy Sample was saying. As Kate watched, Daisy shook her head vehemently and pointed across the patio at a figure hurriedly walking toward the French doors.

Kate and Maggie, feeling invisible behind the sprays of Areca palm that protruded from several pots in front of the bushes, craned their necks to see who it was.

"It's Max," Kate whispered.

"Two nervous setters," Maggie said, using her standard mode of identification. "He's a nice man."

"They don't seem to think so," Kate said, peering between two fronds at the scowling gaggle of shop owners "From the tense look on their faces, Max isn't their favorite person."

"Max was Owen's best friend," Po said. "He's probably taking up Owen's concerns." She got up and looked around the patio. "I think I've had enough."

Maggie and Kate shot up immediately. Maggie pulled her

shoes from beneath the chair and sighed. "They will never fit back on these two sad feet. Not in a million years. Would you all understand?"

Kate and Po's smiles assured Maggie she was among friends. Before the maid could approach them again with more appetizers and wine, the three women, one dangling a pair of high heel shoes from her index finger, slipped through the house and away from Owen Hill's wake. It was a first for her, Kate remarked as she steered her Jeep around the parked cars crowding the street. "The first time I've attended a wake for a murdered man."

And the last, Po hoped fervently.

CHAPTER 6

Tea Leaf

Po needed to get back into her routine. One could think of murder for just so long before it weighed the spirit down lower than a sunken ship. *Come on, girl!* Po thought to herself. Crestwood had a fine police force and they were fully capable of finding the burglar who killed Owen Hill. Or not, as Lucy, her five-year-old granddaughter, would say.

The night before, she had tossed and turned while the wind beat willow branches against her window, trying to figure out this whole mess that was turning Elderberry Road into a sideshow. Any burglar in his right mind was not going to be hanging around Crestwood waiting to be picked up and accused of murdering a prominent, popular man. Would they ever find him and have closure to this? But no matter what the answer was to that question, Po knew one thing for sure: they all had to move on or they'd be reduced to nervous twits. And the best way to do that, in Po's opinion, was to get back to the old routines, for better or for worse.

Po's routine today meant working on her neglected book, a project born of her love for quilting, her passionate belief in the strength of women, and her gift for words. She'd written other books — a biography of Eleanor Roosevelt and a series of young adult books that had received several awards. But this one about women and quilting was special to Po, and writing it was a pleasure, though she sometimes found it difficult to find the time. Steve Jenkins, her editor and friend, would have her head if she didn't get the first draft to him on time. Po pushed the power button on her laptop computer and settled into the leather desk chair while the soft hum of the start-up program filled her cozy den. She dressed for comfort when writing — today in a pair of slim jeans and an old Canterbury College sweatshirt of Sam's. Her hair was loose and smelled slightly of eucalyptus shampoo.

Outside the window a covey of blue jays fought for branch space in the old oak tree. They reminded Po of the brilliant Birds in Flight quilt the Queen Bees had auctioned off last year for the library benefit. Except the birds outside her window weren't flying, poor dears. They didn't know whether to head south for the winter or stay for a while. The warm autumn days had them all confused, but Po for one wasn't complaining. Winter would be here soon enough. And being able to go out for her morning run without piling on several layers was a gift Po wouldn't turn away from.

The familiar clutter of icons filled the computer screen and Po straightened her back, took a drink of coffee, and began to type.

The book came alive beneath her fingers, and when the doorbell sent Hoover flying down the front hall, Po sat still for a moment, her train of thought disappearing into the sound.

How odd, Po thought. Her friends usually stayed away on Wednesdays, knowing that she was probably behind on her writing. With a click of a key, she quickly checked her computer calendar just to make sure she hadn't forgotten a meeting. Those memory lapses seemed to come with increasing frequency these days! Reassured that there wouldn't be a committee of women standing on her steps, Po left her computer and headed for the front door.

Mary Hill stood on the brick steps, holding an empty casserole dish in her hands. She wore a sweater dress the color of liquid gold that flowed over her slender curves like honey. A blue cashmere sweater was wrapped elegantly around her narrow shoulders.

"Hello, Mary," Po said. "What an unexpected pleasure. Come in."

"I'm on my way to Windsor House, Po, but I wanted to drop off your dish and thank you for the shrimp casserole. It was delicious."

Po took the glass dish and ushered Mary through the door. "Well, you can surely spare two minutes from that store,

Mary. We'll have a cup of coffee and you can tell me how you are doing."

"I'm fine, Po," Mary said.

A slight smile softened Mary's face and Po marveled at the beauty that could ride on the heels of terrible grief. Mary Hill was pale, and her sad eyes filled her narrow face. But despite the tragedy of the past week, she was striking to look at.

"Bless Owen for buying Windsor House," Mary continued. "The store is such consolation. His presence is everywhere in it." Her eyes lowered and her voice dropped off. She fingered the knot of her sweater. For a moment, Po thought Mary may have forgotten where she was. Then the moment passed and Mary looked up and smiled again at Po.

It was an odd smile, Po thought. Forced, perhaps, or maybe just a worn-out smile that had seen too much duty in recent days.

"And I have my church, Po. I'd never have been able to get through this without Reverend Gottrey and his wife. Everyone there has been kind and caring beyond belief."

"Mary, you and Owen have been more than generous to that church. We all know that there'd be no roof over their heads — literally — if Owen hadn't stepped in with his gracious giving."

Po led Mary through the wide hallway, its walls filled with framed family pictures — "Po's gallery," Sam had called it — and into the comfortable kitchen at the back of the house.

"Please Mary, have a seat." Po pointed to a chair on the other side of the large trestle table that anchored the center of the long kitchen and family room. For nearly thirty years, the heavy oak table had centered the life of the Paltrow family, bearing the weight of dinners and discussions, of tears and homework and sometimes heated, often humorous debate. "If this table had ears," Po's daughter Sophie often said. And the understated truth in the trailing sentence always made the family laugh.

"This is a wonderful table," Mary said, as if reading Po's thoughts. "With a little refinishing, it could be worth a considerable amount of money. If you ever want to sell it . . ." She took the coffee mug that Po handed her and left the sentence dangling in the coffee-scented air.

Po laughed, though the thought of anyone refinishing her table sliced painfully into her heart. Every pencil mark and wine stain, every dent and rough edge, held a story laced with affection. She wouldn't refinish the table on her life. "This table is like a member of the family," she said out loud, and slid a generous piece of lemon coffeecake onto one of her green depression ware plates. She set it in front of Mary, then served one up for herself and sat down across from her guest.

"Speaking of vintage things," Po said, "How is Windsor House doing? Will you be all right, Mary?"

"All right?" Mary's carefully fashioned eyebrows lifted as one.

"Well, I know from Selma that it's an enormous job owning a shop, especially one as elegant as yours," Po said. "And now that you're the sole owner . . ."

"Owen had his academic career," Mary said simply. "The store was my responsibility. It won't really be that different." She picked at the lemon cake with the tip of her fork.

"And I have Andy Pearson, you know," Mary continued. "He's helped us for a while now and loves being at the store.

Owen kept the books, and he was very involved in our trips to seek new merchandise, so I'll need to think about that. But it will work out, I'm sure of that. Owen loved Windsor House dearly, and if for no other reason, I will make sure it continues to succeed."

"I'm sure you will, Mary. And I didn't mean to indicate otherwise. You've done an amazing job at Windsor House. There isn't another store like it in the whole state."

"No, there isn't," Mary said. "People come from all over, and with some work, I think we can make the rest of the block a draw as well."

Po cradled her coffee mug in her hands and leaned back in the chair. "I'm not sure I understand what you mean, Mary. The Elderberry shops are wonderful. How can you make them more so?"

Mary laughed uncomfortably. "Of course they are all wonderful, Po. I didn't mean to say they weren't. But we — all the shop owners — we have a vision, you see. We share a common goal — to grow our block into a distinguished shopping area, one with a lovely, gracious ambience. An art center ..."

Now Po was the one to laugh, "Oh, Mary," she said. "We love it the way it is. Please don't change a single, solitary thing. The Elderberry shops meet all our needs — lovely antiques and gifts, wine, cheese, and our very own quilting center."

Mary's face showed little emotion. She spoke carefully. "I understand what you're saying, Po. And I didn't mean to suggest that the present shops are not respectable. It's just that, well, you can always make things better, you know."

"Oh, I certainly know that, Mary. Heavens, it's the story of my life. I am on a continual quest to be better." She took another drink of coffee and looked Mary in the eye. "But tell me, Mary Hill, do you really think the neighbors want a block of high-priced stores on Elderberry Road? They can get their fill of that in Kansas City. But the delightful mixture we have here in the neighborhood seems just right. There's something for everyone."

Mary was silent. She seemed to be examining her coffee-cake with undo seriousness. Finally she said, "Maybe, Po. But change is good." She pushed back her chair and reached for her purse.

"Mary, you have a lot to deal with right now, with Owen's death and all the changes forced upon you. Changes to your business should be the last thing on your mind."

"As I said, Po, change is good." Mary's voice was steely.

"Mary, if I have offended you, I'm so sorry."

"Of course you haven't offended me, Po. But taking care of our house, our properties and charities, our store — well, that's my life now. And I will do the best I can to make Owen proud." Mary turned and walked out the front door.
Po stood at the door and watched Mary walk down the porch steps and along the brick sidewalk to the street. Her sleek, elegant car was waiting at the curb. Po watched her slide behind the wheel, then drive slowly off to Windsor House and a day of selling extravagantly priced artifacts to people who didn't need them.

Po frowned. She brushed her hair back behind one ear, her hands on her hips, and shook her head. "Lord," she wondered aloud, "what in heaven's name was that all about?"

CHAPTER 7

Tumbling Blocks

Early the next Saturday, Selma unlocked the door to her quilt shop and ushered the Queen Bees into the back room. A collective sigh of relief hung heavy on the early morning air.

"A giant dose of normal — that's what we need," Phoebe said. She walked over to the far end of the eight-foot table, the spot where she always sat, and dropped her bag to the floor.

"I don't know if we've actually reached normal yet," Selma said. "But by gum we'll be there soon."

"Of course we will," Po said, and settled down at the end of the table. "So let's talk anniversary quilt. This is the day we start in earnest."

"I think Susan and I have it figured out," Leah said. "Tell me what you think." She walked over to the table and held up a diagram — a large page filled with tiny squares.

"This is our version of an old pattern called the Crystal Star. Perfect for Selma, don't you think?" She looked over at Selma.

They all agreed that a star would be good. Even Kate, who expressed great fear that she'd have to master points, thought it was a great idea. "A star for our star," she said, and smiled at Selma.

"The Crystal Star pattern," Susan went on, "was printed in *The Kansas City Star* in the 1930s. It was part of the series they did for all those years, reprinting quilt patterns that people sent in from Nebraska and Kansas and Oklahoma — from the whole center of the country."

"My mother collected every one of those," Eleanor said. "They were a history book in the making."

Po nodded. Her mother collected them, too, then passed them down to Po. She looked over at the diagram. "How will we divide this up?" she asked.

"The quilt will be five blocks square, with several blocks reserved for a special center star, so we'll each have to make at least two. Then the fastest among us can do the remaining ones. We'll set the center star on point and give it its own frame. It will be special, a focal point. If you look at this diagram you can see that it becomes a star within a star, and will take up five blocks. Maybe Susan and I can work on the center while the rest of you do the border stars."

"Will all our stars be the same?" Phoebe asked. Phoebe loved experimenting, no matter what the outcome.

"You can make it as special as you want by changing the center of your star. For example, the middle could be a checkerboard pattern, a diamond, or plain. A small pinwheel would work, too. Live dangerously, Pheebs."

"I have some fabric we can start with," Susan said. "Leah and I picked out these three fabrics for the common colors, based on the color scheme we all agreed on last month. We'll each use these three in our stars in some way. Then everyone can pick coordinating fabrics and work those into their own design." She picked up a purple cotton print. "This will be the common background for all the stars. What do you think?"

"This will be beautiful, Leah," Kate said. "Even with me working on it!"

Selma had gone to the front of the store to wait on a customer. "Frankly, I can't imagine a better time to do this, nor a better person to do it for," Kate said.

The others joined in, excited to get started and eager to honor Selma and Parker's Dry Goods' fiftieth anniversary in this way.

Susan passed out copies of the pattern and piled the table with bolts of fabric in deep shades of blue and purple, pale-yellow prints, blue-black stripes, and lavender and gold. Maggie fingered a deep purple fabric with stripes of black and yellow swirling through it. "It will be a magnificent quilt," she pronounced, and the anniversary project began.

"What's the latest news, Selma?" Kate asked as Selma came back into the room. She reached for a mat and rotary cutter.

Selma rolled her sewing table up to the edge of the work-table and flicked the on switch. The gentle hum of the machine filled the room. "Well, the police have stopped hanging out in my store, which is a good thing. It's not exactly a welcoming, come-hither sight for my customers, what with P.J. in his crisp blue uniform standing guard at the front door."

"P.J. Flanigan?" Kate asked.

"The one and only," Maggie said, and winked at Kate.

"I went to high school with him," Kate explained to the others. "I thought P.J. went into law."

"He did," Phoebe spoke up. "He was in law school with Jimmy. Everyone knew P.J. He's one tall piece of man candy!" Her laughter spun up to the skylight.

"Well, I won't argue with that," Kate grinned mischievously.

"P.J Flanigan is a great guy," Po said. "His parents are dear friends of mine. After law school, P.J. switched to police work, following in his father's footsteps. I suspect he'll go back to law some day." She looked over at Kate. "And if I remember correctly, Kate Margaret Simpson, high school wasn't the only place you went with P.J."

Kate snorted. "A lifetime ago, Po. But P.J. and I had a lot of fun, I must admit."

"He brings his two Aussies to me. And you can tell a master by his dogs, you know," Maggie said. "Kanga and Mocha are the sweetest girls in town."

Po grinned and said, "Kate, you know your mother and I

used to place bets on the comings and goings of P.J. Flanigan — when you two would break up and when you'd make-up. We'd sit on my back porch sipping very dry martinis, always with a thin slice of apple floating on top, and wait for the next soap opera chapter to play itself out."

"Kate — a side of you I didn't know!" Phoebe lifted her eyebrows. "P.J. Flanigan, not bad. Were you part of the in crowd, Katie? I imagine P.J. was quite the hot shot."

Kate made a face and Po laughed, remembering the Kate of a dozen or more years ago. Kate had been her own person even back then, and she wasn't in the popular group — not by a long shot — though she had had plenty of friends. She'd been a wild, beautiful filly, a thorn in her mother's side much of the time, opinionated, stubborn, but underneath it all, a courageous, sweet soul. Po and Meg were almost always proud of Kate, even while they worried about her and wondered what she'd do next to disrupt their peaceful lives.

"P.J. was a hot shot, I guess," Kate admitted. "He played every sport known to man. Me? Well, my best friend Honora liked me. And P.J. did, too. But sorry to disappoint you, Pheebs. You won't find me on the Prom Queen page in the Crestwood High yearbook."

"Speaking of P.J.," Eleanor said, "what does he think about this awful murder business, Selma?"

Selma shook her head. "He said they're still thinking it was a burglary. The 'perp,' as P.J. calls the scum bum who did this, assumed the store would be empty that late at night."

"So what did this guy steal — a bolt of fabric?" Phoebe asked. "That'll provide a great Sun City retirement."

"Now that's a good question, Phoebe," Selma said.

"Whoever this person was, he wasn't the brightest crayon in the box. He took my locked box from under the counter up front. And walked off with a sum total of half a dozen hand-written store charges, some change, and a stack of order sheets I had planned to finish that day. And Owen's wallet and watch, I believe I heard P.J. say."

"Owen died for loose change," Leah said. There was an edge to her usually soft voice. She lined up her cut strips of fabric on the table and smoothed them out with her fingers. "Owen was a good man, a decent man. This whole thing just doesn't make sense."

"No, it doesn't make any sense at all. And I think P.J. Flanigan, as intelligent as he is, is dead wrong," Po said. She blurted the words out with more force than she had intended and was slightly embarrassed when all eyes in the room turned toward her.

Susan, her arms carrying a bolt of fabric, walked through the arch that opened the meeting room to the front section of the store. The silence stopped her in her tracks. "What?" she asked, looking from one surprised face to the next. "What's wrong?"

"Po doesn't think a burglar killed Owen Hill," Phoebe said.

Susan dropped the bolt of cotton and stared at Po. "What are you saying, Po? Of course it's a burglary."

"I don't think any burglar worthy of the name would attempt to rob Selma's store. You've all said the same thing in some shape or form, and that's all that I'm saying. I don't think it makes sense. Not with a busy bookstore down the street, and an antique shop with lamps that cost more than my home. So there, that's it. That's what I think."

"But," Susan rested both hands on the back of the ladder chair and steadied herself. "Do you think someone wanted Professor Hill dead?"

Po wished she hadn't started the conversation. Susan was a sensitive woman and had her own bundle of worries — caring for an ill mother, going back to college at the age of 38, and working as hard as she did to make ends meet. She had also been on edge lately. Po shouldn't have burdened her with another fear beyond her control. "I don't mean to stir things up. Perhaps I spoke out of turn."

"You, Po?" Kate said, her voice lifting at the end of the question, and they all laughed at the affectionate jibe. The tension lifted.

Po shushed Kate with a wave of her hand, but she laughed along with the rest of the Queen Bees. It was true that she sometimes found it difficult to hold her tongue when strong emotion gripped her. And she felt strongly about this issue, mostly because she didn't want her dear friend Selma in any danger. And if someone killed Owen in Selma's store for reasons other than theft, then danger might still lurk there in the jumble of fabric bolts and sewing notions. Po wanted the danger faced, and then erased.

"Well, frankly, it doesn't make sense to me either, Po." Selma picked up a metal can filled with straight pins and handed it to Phoebe who was pinning a strip of bright green polka dot fabric to a lush lavender print. Her star matched her personality to a T, Po had commented earlier — bright, daring, and sparkling.

Selma went on. "I for one could have killed Owen a time or two — of late, he'd been pushing for that fancy brick sidewalk, in spite of my very vocal protests — but I didn't. That's not to say, though, that he might have pushed others far enough that they did."

"There's a lot of gossip brewing around town," Phoebe said. "Even at the park where I take Jude and Emma. Greta Janssen — she has a two-year-old and goes to Reverend Gottrey's church — she said that she thought the Reverend was having a hard time looking sad about the whole thing. Owen Hill was about to pull the plug on the endless donations he and Mary made to the church." She pulled a small ironing board up to the other end of the table and plugged in the iron.

Maggie joined in. "Hans Broker, he lives just a street over." Maggie pointed with her head toward the back window and the large comfortable homes that lay beyond the thick border of bushes. "He had his lab, Sparky, in for shots last week, and he said there'd been activity in this alley on and off for awhile now. Night noises when there shouldn't have been. I guess Sparky barked like crazy a few nights, according to Hans, and then finally got used to it."

"So he heard something on the night Owen died?" Kate asked.

"Well, that's where his story lost a little ground. He wasn't sure about that, and yet it was so warm that night that he must have had his windows open. Everyone did."

Po stood and held a piece of royal purple cotton up to the natural light. It would be perfect for one of her stars. She set it down next to her coffee cup, pleased. "I don't mean to put a damper on Hans' story," she said, focusing back on the conversation. "Hans is a sweet man, but he wears two hearing aids. And at that time of night both of them were probably on his bedside table, right beside his empty glass of Jack Daniels. Now Sparky is credible, but there are a thousand squirrels that live back there, not to mention the beautiful black cat that I ran into that awful morning." Po sat down and fingered the fabric in front of her.

"Those night-time noises could have been made by Wesley Peet," Selma said.

"The security guard?" Kate asked. She sat down at Selma's machine and pushed the pedal, stitching together the small rectangles and squares that would be her flying geese — the rays of her star. "He's one creepy dude. He skulks around in the shadows and rarely speaks. Honestly, he scares me, Selma."

"He's frightening," Susan agreed. She had slipped into a chair and was helping Eleanor line up her fabric against a paper template. Eleanor had decided to paper piece, insisting that the points of her star would be absolutely perfect. "Wesley is usually around when I'm closing up." She held the template and fabric up to the light to make sure the alignment was perfect. Her unfinished thought hung there in the air awkwardly.

Selma took a pin out of her mouth. "Wesley's an odd duck, that's true. The ESOC hired him last year after that unfortunate incident with Susan."

All eyes turned toward Susan, who paled at the attention.

Selma went on. "Some guy began to harass Susan as she was closing up the store late one night. Thank God for Max Elliott. He was working in his office across the street and heard the ruckus." Selma looked at her assistant again.

"As quiet as Susan seems, there's a tigress beneath that Grace Kelly facade. She made plenty of noise. Anyway, Max rushed out and chased the fellow off. Then he went to Owen, and the next thing we knew, we had our very own Elderberry Road security guard."

"Max is a good man," Susan said in a soft voice.

"I agree that Wesley's a peculiar sort, but he seems harmless enough. His bulk alone would frighten anyone off, so he doesn't need to do much. He's noisy, though, so he could very well be the cause of Sparky's barking," Selma said.

"I think he sometimes has a nip or two," Susan said.

"Or five or six. In fact, he recently fell right smack onto a garbage can. Smashed the side in flatter than a pancake. We were having our 'sweat-sock' meeting that night and he scared the life out of us. Owen was fit to be tied. He threatened to fire him. In fact, I think he would have, if . . ." Her words fell off. "If he hadn't been killed" hung in the still air.

"Maybe someone should fire him," Kate said.

"He's better than nothing," Selma answered. "And I think Owen overreacted. There've been times when I've been glad to see Wesley standing in the alley while I got safely inside my car. And as clumsy as he can be, he's a warm body. A big noisy one, but a body."

"Speaking of noisy, those ESOC meetings could have been what Hans heard," Susan said. "They get kind of noisy, and you were meeting that night."

"We do get noisy sometimes," Selma agreed. "I guess we can be a cantankerous group."

"What do you talk about?" Kate asked. She looked at the two small triangles she had stitched together and frowned at the misaligned point. Slowly, she began to pull the stitching out. As the least experienced quilter, Kate had chosen the easiest star center for her block. But points, Kate had learned, were difficult, no matter what.

"We talk about everything," Selma said. "Hiring security guards, repairing roofs, fixing rain gutters. Insurance."

"Owen was one of your directors?" Eleanor asked. She had come back into the room, leaning lightly on her hand-carved cane, after exploring Selma's new delivery of hand-died batiks. She sat down at an empty spot near Kate.

"Yes, he was," Selma said. "We elect three directors so we don't all have to meet on every tiny detail. This year it was Owen, Daisy, and Ambrose. We're meeting soon to select someone to take Owen's place."

"Would you be a candidate, Selma?" Po asked.

"Not on your sweet life, Po. You've been around long enough to know all these folks on the block. Decisions don't come by us easily and the less involved I have to be, the better. I have my hands full keeping up this shop. Besides, I detest those meetings. The group meets far more than I can stomach, and if you're a director, you meet even more often."

"But surely you have a say in what decisions are made regarding the shops, don't you?" The thought of Ambrose Sweet and some of the others making decisions that affected Selma's store bothered Po.

"Selma should have the biggest say." Susan spoke up before Selma could answer. "We have the most frontage, and when they decide about snow removal and sidewalk repair and window awnings, well, it affects us financially more than some of the others."

Tumbling Blocks

Po noticed Susan's use of "we" and she smiled to herself. That was good. Selma needed someone else who cared as much about the store as she did. Someone to carry that burden of care and attention.

"Why should you have to pay more, Po?" Kate asked.

"Well, it's the way it works. Each of the owners pays a certain amount into the CAM fund — that's legal gibberish for community area maintenance. The amount we pay is based on square footage, and with all my storage space and having both front and side windows, well, we have a lot of square footage and a lot of frontage . . ."

A noise from the front room broke off her sentence. From the table Susan and Selma could see into the shop and could hear the jingle of the door when new customers came in. Susan stood at the sound of the bell and motioned to Selma that she'd help the customer.

"So when you put in these skylights . . ." Phoebe pointed up to the long narrow windows in the ceiling, ". . . who paid for that? Did it come out of the CAM funds?" Phoebe asked.

"Not those. I put those skylights in a long time ago, when Po came to me and said that we needed to start a quilting circle. And it needed to be held in this very room, and if I didn't add some natural light, we'd all be blind as bats in short order."

Po laughed and Selma continued. "That was long before the Elderberry shop owners got together and decided to buy this block of shops and run it the right way.

"So no, the CAM funds didn't pay for those windows. I did. But things are afoot now that might be beyond my control. Ambrose and Jess, for example, want to put in a brick sidewalk. Mary Hill wants it, too, and was pressuring Owen to see that it happened. He was going along with it — could have killed him for that. That kind of thing will affect me greatly. In fact, it may be the last straw . . ." Selma's voice dropped off as if she had driven off the side of a cliff. She paused for a minute, took a deep breath to collect herself, then looked intently at the small pieces of fabric on the table in front of her. "Fiddlesticks! See what I've done? I've pinned the wrong pieces together. My star will look more like a Drunkard's Path."

Po sensed Selma's distress. She stood and walked over to the handsome oak sideboard that stood beneath the back window. Selma had found it at a flea market and refinished it. It was usually filled with stacks of fabric, jars of scissors, transparent rulers and rotary cutters, and the cupboard below was jammed full of additional supplies. But on Saturday mornings a space in the center was cleared for pots of hot coffee and platters of cinnamon rolls, coffeecake, or whatever delicacies Kate had pulled from her oven a short while earlier. Since she'd joined the group, Po swore their collective weight had risen one hundred percent. She lifted the foil off the platter and breathed in the sweet smells of butter and fresh fruit. "Okay, ladies, it's time for Kate's blueberry scones," she announced.

"Let me help you, Po." Susan came through the archway and moved around the table to Po's side. "Another ten-pound Saturday, compliments of Kate," she said, picking a crumb from the edge of the platter. She took the coffeepot from Po and began to fill the line of mugs.

Po watched Susan pour the coffee. Each Saturday Susan

opened up a little more, relaxed and laughed with all of them. Her blue eyes spoke of a life that wasn't always easy, and Po was glad to see she had some outlet, at least, besides her classes and caring for her mother.

"Watch your squares, everyone. Blueberries stain in the worst way," Kate said.

"Kate, these are amazing," Maggie said, licking a smear of purple from the tip of her finger. "You're going to put Marla out of business."

"That'll be the day." Kate laughed. "This is therapy, pure and simple. It's what I do to forget that three promising young kids in my English class are clearly more interested in pot than Shakespeare, and refuse to listen to my eloquent words of wisdom. Or when I suspect a confused and frustrated fourteen-year-old is about to run away from home, or when I have forty papers to correct and an exam in my own classes the next day, it's when, well, you get the picture. When stressed, I bake." Kate's substitute teaching was a great help in paying for her computer graphics classes at Canterbury College. And she loved the kids. But sometimes it was more than one day and one body could handle nicely.

"Speaking of blueberry scones," Leah said, "feast your eyes on this fabric that Selma found at market." She held up a length of printed fabric. Tiny yellow and green lines meandered across a deep purple background. And at uneven intervals, a bright pinpoint of white lit up the fabric like a starry night.

"Cool," Phoebe said, reaching over to touch the fabric. "It would be amazing in the anniversary quilt."

"The yellow print in my star would look perfect with it,"

Eleanor said.

Po set her empty coffee cup on the side table and watched the shared pleasure light up faces and flow around the table like a sweet summer breeze — and all over a piece of cotton fabric. She watched Selma's eyes deepen to ocean green and the blush return to Susan's high cheekbones. She saw Eleanor's stately shoulders relax as she set a strip of her bright green square on top of the purple, and she watched Maggie and Phoebe's wide smiles as they fingered the fabric with near reverence.

Kate stood next to Po, her arms folded across her chest. She inclined her head toward Po, touching her head lightly with her own. "My dear Po," she said quietly.

Po looked over at her. "What?"

"I see that look on your face, watching these ladies you've pulled together for whatever reason. Mom used to call you 'the gatherer' because you gather people together. You're as soft as marshmallow fluff. And that's just one of the things I love about you." She looped one arm around Po's shoulder. "And I agree with what that look on your face says. It is kind of amazing how a piece of fabric can cover up all the ugliness of this past week."

Po reached out and squeezed Kate's hand. She nodded. But it was more than the fabric, she knew. It was what a quilting bee did for each of these special women, binding their lives together as surely and securely as if they had the same blood running through their veins.

A jingling bell sliced through the moment.

Before either Selma or Susan could make it to the front to greet the customer, P.J. Flanigan appeared in the doorway.

His head nearly touched the top of the arch and a smile as big as Texas softened the strong bones of his face.

"We caught him, ladies," he said proudly. "You can rest easy now. Owen Hill's killer is in jail."

◆

CHAPTER 8

Next Door Neighbor

An hour later, Kate and Po sat at a table in the bay window of Marla's small bakery and café, munching on a late lunch of avocado and brie sandwiches and drinking strong green tea that Marla claimed would add twenty years to one's life. They'd managed to get a little more quilting in after P.J.'s pronouncement and quick exit, but concentration didn't come easily, and the session ended early.

"Selma looked like she shed ten years in those few minutes," Po said. "She was more worried about all this than she let on."

Kate nodded and the two continued to munch on their sandwiches, thoughts of the last week playing in their heads.

Finally Kate broke the silence.

"So, are you convinced?"

Po laughed. Kate was a true kindred spirit and there were times, like right this moment, that she knew Kate could read her thoughts.

"Well, maybe I was wrong," Po said. She smiled over the edge of her teacup. "Maybe it was a burglar, and maybe they caught him."

Kate wiped a dollop of mustard from the corner of her mouth with her napkin. "You know, Po, the whole thing seems odd to me, too. This must be one dimwitted fellow." She chewed her sandwich thoughtfully.

Marla shuffled her way over to their table. The bakery owner's bulk made it difficult to squeeze between the tables, and Po was reminded again that she must convince Marla to get on some kind of a weight loss program or she would surely die before she turned fifty. And then where would they all be? Absolutely no one on earth could match Marla's cheese soufflé nor her homemade, seven-grain bread.

"So," Marla said, leaning over the small table. Her pudgy fingers formed a tent on the tabletop. "I hear they caught the rat who did this to Owen." Her blue-black hair was parted in the middle and pulled back severely, fastened at her neck with a thick rubber band.

"That's what P.J. tells us, Marla. I guess we'll all sleep better tonight," Po said.

"Where'd they catch him?" Marla stood straight and wiped her hands on the smudged apron that wrapped around her middle.

"Out at the Wal-Mart on the other side of town. Apparently he tried to use Owen's credit card. And when the police got there, they discovered he was wearing Owen's Rolex watch."

"Geez! Not a very bright kid, I'd say."

"Well, that's what we thought, too," Po said. "But P.J. says he's not a dummy. And not a kid. The fellow claims he found the wallet and watch in a sack out at the truck plaza near the highway."

"Likely story."

"That's what the police think, too," Kate said. She looked down at the crumbs on her empty plate. "Marla, these avocado sandwiches are great."

Marla beamed. Keeping up with the college crowd and vegetarian eating trends had plunged her into a whole new domain. "Thanks, Katie. If I can satisfy you kids coming back from fancy places like Boston, then I must be doing something right." She turned back to Po. "So has Selma settled down? She was in such a twit about all this."

"Selma's fine, Marla. I think that finding the body of a dear friend in one's back door might put any of us in a twit."

"Friends? Selma and Owen weren't friends, at least not lately. He was pushing to have a brick sidewalk put in all along this street. That would have been bad news — big time — for Selma."

"I understood it was Ambrose and Jesse who were pushing for that."

"Well, sure, them. They think they control taste in this neighborhood. The arbiters of taste, Daisy calls them. But I know for a fact that Mary Hill agreed with them and thought the brick sidewalk would look mighty good outside her fancy store. And she had Owen wrapped around her little finger when it came to that high-falootin' store of theirs."

"I see," Po said, not wishing to pursue the topic further. Marla had mastered the fine art of gossip as carefully as her recipe for cheese soufflé. She also had a reputation for confusing facts, which made her tongue dangerous.

"So how's that quilt coming along for Selma? That's a nice thing you're doing for her."

"It's coming fine," Kate said. "It's a beautiful pattern, and we each get to add our own artistic bits to it. They're even letting me, Marla, believe it or not."

"Well, you better hurry with it, Katie, or Selma may not have a store to hang it in. Business down at that end of the block is slow, I hear," Marla said. "People are a little leery of shopping at a murder scene. And then there's the ugly talk."

A young woman behind the counter called out for Marla to check the rye bread before it came out of the oven. Marla shook her round head in exasperation. "Can't get anyone to do anything around here." Then with a wiggly wave of her fingers, she lumbered back to the kitchen, her thick white soles making squishy sounds on the linoleum floor.

Kate looked longingly at Po's half-finished sandwich.

Po pushed it across the table. "Help yourself, sweetie. Marla has a way of curbing my appetite." Po pushed herself back from the table and crossed her legs. She brushed a crumb off her jeans and watched with pleasure as Kate finished off the rest of her sandwich. Flaky white sprouts escaped from between the slices of whole wheat bread and floated to the table. It amazed Po that any one person could eat as much as Kate did and still be as slender and agile as a young doe.

"What was all that talk about Selma's store?" Kate asked.

"I don't know. But it's probably nothing. What could people possibly be saying about Selma? She's one of the finest, most hardworking women I know. Raised two children all by herself, put them both through college, and she runs that store with a business brain that rivals Bill Gates." Po glanced at her watch. "Katie, dear, if you're about done, I think I need to move on into my day. My Saturday list is wearing a hole in my purse."

"I'm ready, Po." Kate placed her napkin on the table and drained her teacup. She slipped her arms into a jeans jacket and walked across the room.

They paid their bill and moved toward the front door, made almost invisible by the sunshine streaming through the glass. Just as Kate was about to push it open, a huge shadow filled the doorframe, blocking their exit. P.J. Flanigan stood on the other side. He slowly pulled the door open. The same wide grin that Kate remembered from her high school algebra class filled his face.

"Katie Simpson. I knew I recognized that ornery stance back there in the quilt shop. Were you hiding from me behind those bolts of fabric? Why didn't you announce yourself? Fess up and apologize!"

"Apologize? And what would that be for, P.J.?" Kate asked.

Next Door Neighbor

P.J. had been a year ahead of her in school, so he must be thirty, thirty-one now, Kate figured — and as she looked him up and down, she decided the years had settled on him very nicely. His strong-boned face had lost the roundness of a younger P.J., the wide set eyes had mellowed to a rich hazel, and that amazing smile that she remembered well had warmed over the years.

"Well, for going off to Wellesley, for one thing — and then for not coming back — oh, yeah, and for breaking my heart." He clutched his chest and swayed back and forth, his eyes never leaving her face.

"You're blocking traffic, P.J.," Po said sternly. "Marla will have you stripped of that shiny badge if you turn a paying customer away."

P.J. took a step backward holding the door open for Kate and Po. He followed them to the sidewalk and planted a kiss on Po's cheek. "And a hello to you, too, my lovely Po. I swear you get prettier every time I see you."

Po gave him a quick hug. "Useless mush, but I love it. And much as I'd like to stand here and soak up your foolish talk, I have things to do and people to see. So I'm off. Kate, toodles. As for you, P.J. Flanigan, keep the peace."

She left them standing there together, and wondered briefly when they'd discover that Po was P.J.'s god-mother, too. Surely less important connections had b-rought two young people together. She began to hum and looked up at the sky. It was a bright, sunshiny day.

CHAPTER 9

Monkey Wrench

Po walked down the street at a steady clip. She paused to admire Ambrose and Jesse's window display of wines and distilled spirits, their colorful, carefully designed labels presented like works of fine art. Mounds of imported cheeses on wooden platters, baskets of French bread and crackers, and a tasteful arrangement of Riedel wine glasses painted a portrait as pretty as any gallery. The owners had finally been licensed to open a small wine bar inside the shop, and Po could see several people sitting at round bistro tables, eating a wine and cheese lunch in the back of the store. Wine at noon would encourage a sound nap, she thought. A martini at sunset served her much better.

She continued on, glancing at the lopsided window boxes outside Daisy's flower shop. Several limp ferns surrounded a display of plastic roses. Oh dear. Daisy had beautiful fresh flowers inside but the outside display wouldn't exactly entice customers. Perhaps she could subtly suggest that Daisy fix the rotted wood and then fill the boxes with those gorgeous bronze mums that sat in a row inside the shop.

When Po reached Windsor House Antiques, she turned and looked back down Elderberry Road. Kate and P.J. were still standing beneath the black street lamp outside Marla's shop. P.J.'s head was inclined slightly, leaning into Kate's space. He was listening intently. Kate had a pleased look on her face and her hands were moving, punctuating her words.

Filling in the years, Po supposed. They still made a handsome couple, even after all this time had passed. Lord, wouldn't she and Meg have had a wonderful time mulling it all over, conjecturing, spinning dreams. A sudden pang of loneliness washed through Po as swiftly as a fast-moving stream. She straightened her shoulders and sighed, resigned to life's unpredictable twists and turns, and walked on into Mary Hill's antique store.

A small group of women, dressed in tailored jackets and wool slacks, their arms heavy with Windsor House shopping bags and boxes tied with thick gold braid, made their way out of the store. Po smiled at the women as they exited, knowing that they were probably from Kansas City or Topeka, not natives, and were visiting Crestwood for the day.

Or perhaps they were in town to take their college students to lunch after indulging in extravagant shopping at Windsor House. Mary was right — she was drawing people from all over to her small, tasteful shop.

Po looked around, her eyes adjusting to the soft light cast by accent lamps and small spots aimed at ornately framed paintings. Mary Hill was sitting at a small curved desk on the far side of the shop, writing on a small pad of paper. She looked up and spotted Po at the same time Po saw her and smiled broadly. Po was relieved at the welcome smile. The uncomfortable conversation they'd had a few days ago must be forgotten.

Mary stood and hurried over to Po. "Oh, Po, if you haven't shown up at just the perfect time."

"So you've heard?" Po asked.

Mary nodded. "That dear P.J. came by with the news."

"P.J. stopped in to tell Selma, too. I wanted to be sure you were all right, Mary."

Mary took Po's hand and clasped it tightly. "Po, I'm so relieved, so proud of our fine police force. So anxious to put this all behind me."

"And they told you they found Owen's watch on the man?" Po searched Mary's face. How difficult this whole ordeal must be for her. "It's such an awful thought — that Owen lost his life for . . . for nothing. It's certainly beyond reason."

"The watch was expensive," Mary said. "An anniversary gift. Perhaps the man knew that. Knew that Owen would have money and valuables on him."

"Maybe he did," Po said, nodding. "But a watch? A watch

for the life of a wonderful man? It's such a terrible waste."

"Yes." Mary's eyes filled, and Po pulled a clean tissue from the pocket of her suede jacket. "It will get easier, Mary, I promise you that."

Mary nodded and dabbed at her delicate nose. "I know it will, Po. Thank you. I appreciate everything you've done, too. Your friendship has meant a great deal to me during this difficult time."

Po smiled but held her silence. She and Mary were certainly very familiar with one another, having mingled at college functions when Sam was president and Owen a professor, and from the very fact of living in the same small town for many years. But she had never considered Mary a friend, really, and realized with some sadness that she didn't even know who Mary's friends were, or if she had any. Mary always stayed close to Owen at college functions, a beautiful shadow at his side, rarely joining the vivacious cluster of female faculty and spouses who seemed drawn to one another while the men retreated to smoke their cigars. That overt dependence must make Owen's death doubly difficult for Mary, Po thought. She determined then and there to make more of an effort to include her in dinner parties and maybe even invite her to a play or concert this fall. Po seemed to have season tickets to more events than days in the year.

"While I'm here, I wondered if you could help me with a gift, Mary. It's a birthday gift for a favorite aunt of mine. I was thinking of a small picture frame or vase. Nothing elaborate."

"Of course." Mary had resumed her composed, business-woman persona and smiled at Po. "We will find the perfect thing."

Po looked around the store. Every inch was filled to over-flowing with exquisite items — armoires, brocade-covered Queen Anne chairs, crystal chandeliers that had once ador-ned British manor houses, and handsome Baroque mirrors. The scent of lacquered wood, lemon and linseed oil, and the expensive perfume of customers hung heavy in the air. A tall glass display case near Mary's work desk caught Po's eye. "How absolutely beautiful," she said, walking over to the lit case.

Each thick glass shelf of the cabinet displayed several glass paperweights, their blown globes filled with complex designs — clusters of complex millefiori, tiny canes of exquisite color fused together in clear, perfect crystal balls.

"This collection is my pride and joy," Mary said. "Aren't they beautiful? Owen and I look for them whenever we go abroad or to auctions."

Po started at the use of the present tense, but Mary went on, not catching herself.

"We've been collecting them for awhile now, but the dis-play case just came yesterday. See this?" She pointed to an antique Baccarat ball with a white carpet background of sparkling white stardust canes. The canes stood out like gems. "Each paperweight is so distinct, so beautiful in its own way. I could look at them for hours."

"These are amazing, Mary." Po glanced at the $15,000 price tag. "But surely not something Aunt Peg needs for her night-stand!"

Mary laughed. "The price range is vast. It depends on a lot of things — whether the piece is from the classic period, the clarity of glass, whether it's signed. And there are forgeries, of course. But even the less expensive balls can be works of art. They're like quilts, in a way." Mary pointed to one in the middle of the shelf. Circular millefiori garlands floated in a green flash paperweight. In the center was a complex arrow cane, encircled by a ring of stardust canes, and surrounded by six spaced garlands, each with a complex cane center.

Po leaned forward and examined the design carefully.

"Yes, I can see that, Mary. There is great similarity in the joining together of tiny pieces to make a work of art. And even the designs are similar, the intricate pieces making up a whole flower."

"You should bring the Queen Bees in some day to see them. A field trip."

"I'll do that. Or at least send them over on their own. And in the meantime, I think I shall have you wrap up that lovely brass picture frame for my favorite aunt and be about my day." She pointed to a small, tasteful frame sitting on a table-top.

"That is a good choice, Po. We'll save the paperweight for another day."

Po laughed heartily. "Like the day I win the lottery," she said.

Outside, the city of Crestwood was wide-awake and bathed in bright mid-day sunshine. P.J. and Kate were gone, but the sidewalk was filled with Saturday shoppers, moving in and out of the Elderberry shops. Recently the shop owners had added several benches to the area, positioning them up and down the block, fastened securely in concrete. They added a quaint touch, and Po wondered if this was the first step toward the brick sidewalk that Selma was dreading.

A few storefronts down, Po spotted Ambrose Sweet, out side his shop. He was sitting on one of the benches talking with an enormous man in a dark blue jacket. The man looked familiar to Po, even though he was sitting sideways and she couldn't see his face. The sheer bulk of his frame and the slouch of his massive shoulders made him stand out. As she neared the bench, she was amused at the contrast between the two men. Ambrose Sweet probably gardened in his carefully pressed wool slacks and cashmere sweater. Po couldn't imagine him in any other attire.

And the enormous, disheveled man sitting next to him, though wearing some sort of a uniform, looked like someone who had spent time "on the road," as Sam used to say.

"Good morning, Po," Ambrose said as she approached the two men.

Po smiled and waited for the other man to turn her way. He moved slowly because his heavy body didn't pivot easily on the bench. When he turned toward her, Po took a step backwards, then stopped and regained her composure. She'd seen him from a distance plenty of times. But not up close like this, not nearly close enough to be assaulted by the stench of sweat and alcohol that radiated off his heavy blue security uniform. One front tooth was darkened with decay, the other slightly crooked. His lips puffed out and a small round chin seemed totally disproportionate to the massive face that housed it.

Susan and Kate and the others were right.

Wesley Peet was a frightening man.

CHAPTER 10

Falling Timbers

This would probably be the last Sunday that she and Leah would be able to walk down to Elderberry Road without bundling up, Po guessed. Today she was comfortable in her yellow sweatshirt and soft pants, but in no time flat she'd be bundled up to her nose in heavy down. She walked at a steady clip, breathing in the solid earthy smell of autumn. Layers of leaves crunched beneath her running shoes and in the distance she smelled a hint of sage burning in a fireplace somewhere.

Just ahead of her, at the junction of Elderberry and Oak, Po spotted Leah. She was sitting on a bench in a tiny triangle of green that marked the beginning of Elderberry Road.

Leah stood and waved. She wore one of her signature earth-toned gauzy dresses that brushed her ankles as she walked. On Leah, it looked elegant and chic rather than a throwback to the '70s, as did her leather sandals and long, beaded earrings. A bright multi-colored scarf tied loosely around her shoulders completed her look. Po suspected that Leah's unique, arresting appearance caused many a coed to change their dress style, at least for those weeks that they sat mesmerized in Leah's semester-long course.

Po and Leah had begun their Sunday morning tradition over a decade ago when their husbands discovered they were great golf partners and that late Sunday morning was the perfect time to indulge their habit. Po and Sam met the younger couple at a fall faculty tea where new professors were introduced to the rest of the Canterbury College family. Leah was the new Yale PhD, recruited to put together a women's studies program in a school that was still shaking off its all-male influence. Her husband was the town's new pediatrician. Although Canterbury had been co-ed for at least a dozen years, change came slowly, and Po knew that the then thirty-year-old Leah Sarandon would have her hands full. Leah surprised everyone, though, including Po. Hidden beneath her gentle beauty and quiet way was a steely strength that came through at that very first tea when she challenged several tenured professors to an animated discussion on the role of women in settling the state. Po determined then and there that she and the young woman would be friends.

The Paltrows invited Leah and Tim over soon after and almost immediately, despite the difference in ages, the foursome discovered shared passions that went beyond the game of golf: cross-country skiing, hiking in Colorado's Gore Range, heated political and literary discussions, and — for Po and Leah — a love and appreciation for the fine art of quilting. Po brought Leah to a Queen Bees gathering shortly after and she'd been an integral part of the group ever since. Po met Leah at the corner with a quick hug and the two women crossed the street quickly, driven by growling stomachs and anticipation of Marla's breakfasts.

Po waved at an elderly couple who lived just down the street from her. Only Elderberry Books and Marla's Bakery and Café were open for business on Sunday mornings, but in nice weather people gathered leisurely, not going anywhere, content to greet neighbors after church, catch up on their reading in one of the old leather chairs in Gus's book store, or chat in small groups waiting for their name to be called for a table at Marla's. Today a line of people crowded the sidewalk outside the café, waiting for an empty table.

"A half-hour wait," someone called out as Po and Leah approached.

"Perfect timing," Po said. "Mary Hill has the most remarkable paper weight display in her shop. Maybe we can catch a peek through the window while we wait."

The two strolled down the street, walking in and out of patches of bright sunshine and savoring the cool crisp fall air.

They moaned in unison as they passed Daisy's plastic flowers display. "I swear they're growing," Leah murmured.

Po laughed. "Owen was assigned the task of telling Daisy to shape this up, I hear. She was fit to be tied."

"Daisy's wrath is scary," Leah said. She looked up ahead at the brick front of Windsor House Antiques. Small green awnings shielded the windows from the bright sunshine.

"I hear Mary is back at work."

"It's the best thing for her, I think." Po stepped close to the plate glass window and looked in at the display of vases and desk lamps. Beyond the window the shop was nearly dark except for several small security lights. Po pointed toward the new cabinet by Mary's desk. "The paper weight display is over there."

Leah cupped her hands around her eyes and peered into the store. "Oh, my — even from here, I can see how beautiful they are," she said. "Tim bought me a Perthshire weight when I graduated. It's one of the loveliest things I own. I'll definitely be back to see Mary's collection when the store is open."

Leah turned to go when Po stepped back to the window, wrinkled her forehead, and looked intently through the smudged window glass. "I saw movement," she said, and motioned for Leah to look. A sliver of unexpected fear circled Po.

Leah peered through the glass. "It's just Mary, Po."

As Po's eyes adjusted to the darkness inside the store, she could see her, too. Mary Hill was standing at the opposite side of the store, nearly hidden from view by a large armoire and a hanging tapestry. Po frowned. "I think there's someone with her."

A man stepped out of the shadow of the armoire and

moved slowly toward Mary. He was medium height, not much taller than Mary, but his face was hidden from view.

Po raised her hand, ready to knock on the window and scare him away. But before she could move, the man handed Mary something. It looked from the window to be a handful of papers. Mary took them and looked down at the white sheets. The man stood by quietly while Mary stared at the papers. Even from a distance, Po could see the vacant, sad look on her face.

Before the two women could pull themselves away, Mary's narrow shoulders slumped and her small body seemed to collapse in on itself. The papers fell from her fingers and floated to the floor.

"Po, does she need our help?" Leah whispered. "What's happening?"

"I can't tell, but he doesn't seem to be threatening."

Then the man bent over and gathered the papers scattered on the floor. He stood and slipped the papers into a briefcase.

Mary's eyes were lowered and her face seemed shadowed in grief. The man set the briefcase on the floor and took her in his arms in a gentle embrace. Mary didn't respond, and the man stepped back, his head lowered. He looked like he was trying to console her or help her with her sadness. He pulled a white handkerchief out of his pocket and handed it to Mary.

"Who is that?" Leah whispered.

"There's something familiar about him. The way he stands, maybe?"

"Whoever he is, she seems okay with him being there, don't you think?"

Po pulled back from the window and pushed a handful of

hair behind her ear. "Yes. And I'm beginning to feel guilty, standing here like this. Poor Mary. She was probably down here to deal with her grief in private, and here she is, on a stage instead."

"I agree. And my stomach can't hold out much longer. Let's eat."

They glanced through the window once more to assure themselves that everything was all right. Mary was sitting in a chair now, and the person with her was leaning over her, talking quietly. She seemed more composed and was looking intently at the man.

"She seems to be in good hands, whoever he is," Po said. They turned and headed down the street. "It's good to know Mary has people to help her through this. Sometimes she seems so alone."

"It couldn't have been easy for her being married to Owen. He was involved in a million things at the college, and I don't think they interested Mary very much."

"But she certainly stood at his side at all those faculty events. And if you'll pardon me for saying so, Leah, those things could be dryer than your martinis."

"And they still are." Leah laughed. "You adapt."

The crowd had thinned in front of the cafe, and Marla waved them in.

"Where've you two been?" she scolded and ushered them to a table near the window. "Thought you weren't coming. I might have sent the National Guard after you. It wouldn't be Sunday if you two ladies didn't show up."

"You know we can't go more than a week without one of your breakfasts, Marla," Leah said.

"That's a fact. Sit down and I'll have Stella pour you some coffee. Eggs'll be ready in two shakes of a lamb's tail." She wiped her hands on a dirty white apron that bulged out from her waste like an awning. "It's been busier than a Macy's sale in here this morning."

"Mostly the church crowd?" Leah asked.

"Yup. And quite the happy crowd today, at least the ones from Reverend Gottrey's church. Too bad I don't have a liquor license — there'd have been many Bloody Mary takers."

"Why's that, Marla?" Po smiled her thanks to Stella as she filled two blue mugs with Marla's special blend coffee.

"You haven't heard?" Marla's face lit up like the sky on the Fourth of July.

Leah and Po glanced quickly at each other. Nothing brightened Marla's disposition faster than the chance to pass along juicy news or gossip.

"Heard what?" Po asked half-heartedly. She wouldn't have asked, but that could have been worse. No one ever knew what would trip Marla's tongue.

"Reverend Gottrey announced at today's service, right directly from the pulpit, that Mary Hill was donating the Hill farm — all eleven hundred acres of it — to the Crestwood All Holy Saints Church."

"What a generous gift," Po said. She knew the land, a wooded haven hidden between well-tended farms and rolling wheat fields just a short drive from Crestwood. She and Sam had been guests at the farm a number of times. Owen Hill had loved the place dearly. He told Po once that it was the one place he could putter and play and be completely at ease. He had a tool shed, an old truck, and lots of fences that always needed fixing. Sometimes he hosted faculty events in the sprawling rustic home on the property. And sometimes Owen had friends out just to enjoy the peace.

Po remembered one day especially, a sunny, snowy day shortly before Sam died. Owen invited the two of them out to cross-country ski. She couldn't remember now how it all came about, how Owen had discovered her love of skiing. But somehow he had and for hours the three of them had skied across the expanse of rolling white fields, in and out of narrow snow-padded paths through the quiet woods. She remembered the still beauty that enveloped them. Po rubbed her arms as the force of memory wrapped around her and squeezed her heart. It had been a cherished day, finished in front of a fire with hot buttered rum, soft jazz playing in the background, Sam at her side — and Owen a humorous, delightful host. A special day.

"Po?" Leah said.

Po looked up. She blinked the present back into focus. "I'm sorry." She wrapped her fingers around the coffee mug and let the warmth seep into her hands. "I was swept up by a host of lovely memories of that farm. Reverend Gottrey's church is very fortunate."

"Fortunate and then some," Marla said. "That place is a huge hunk of prime real estate. Worth a small fortune, according to the mayor. He was in here after church with the wife and those two pretty daughters of his, and he said that everyone in the whole church gasped right out loud when it was announced. The mayor said he sure wished he'd have gotten his wish list in before the Reverend did. City could have used all that land for a park or something."

Po and Leah settled back and sipped their coffee. Marla was on a roll. There was no telling when they'd get their eggs.

"Mary Hill was at church, too. Gracious, the mayor said. Gorgeous, his wife said. She's a pretty lady, that's clear.

"And here's the clincher," Marla continued. Her fingers pressed down on the tabletop forming a fat pink tent. She took a deep breath, then said dramatically, "It'll be called the Owen Hill Spiritual Retreat." Marla stood straight and moved her hands to her heavy hips. She shook her head. Her chins moved back and forth in slow motion. "Owen's Spiritual Ranch, now what do you think of that?"

Po ignored the question. She wasn't sure what Marla was getting at but suspected she was insinuating that Owen wasn't a very religious person. But there was something more pressing than Marla's innuendoes on her mind. "Did you say Reverend Gottrey announced it today, Marla?" she asked.

"Yep. At the early service today."

"And Mary Hill was there?" What she and Leah had just seen didn't mirror a joyful woman announcing a generous memorial gift. That should have been such a special time for Mary.

"In the front pew in one of her expensive suits. The Reverend talked about how generous it all was. The mayor said it embarrassed her some, all that attention, but she was gracious afterwards when they all gathered on the steps outside and thanked her. And he said she looked better than she has since, well, since it all happened — not so pale and skinny, and she was smiling again."

Before Po or Leah could comment, a customer two tables

over insisted he talk to Marla immediately. His wife's eggs were gummy, he announced loudly, a comment Marla wasn't about to take nicely. She lurched her huge body in his direction and prepared to challenge the complaint.

Po looked at Leah across the steam of her coffee. "Well, something stole Mary's smile between church and the Elderberry shop. Either that or she has a double."

"Maybe it was the memories it stirred up?" Leah suggested. "People probably besieged her with kind words and stories about Owen after the service."

"And sent her into a tailspin of grief. It doesn't take much. That's probably exactly what happened."

Stella appeared at the table, her thin arms and long skinny fingers balancing two heaping plates of the Sunday special. Stella was as taciturn as Marla was chatty. She placed the plates on the table and disappeared without a word on her tiny, cat-like feet.

The sweet smell of fresh tarragon and butter rose up on the warm steam.

Leah closed her eyes and leaned into the smell. "Delicious," she whispered.

Po took a forkful of eggs and confirmed it. Marla was an amazing cook. And she assumed that everyone's appetite matched her own. In addition to the eggs, the plates were heaped with crisp strips of bacon, thick hunks of buttered whole-wheat toast, pan-fried potatoes, and a small mountain of fresh fruit topped with a dollop of yogurt. A basket of jams and jellies and goblets of freshly squeezed orange juice completed the feast.

Po and Leah ate in comfortable silence. Outside the window, leaves danced across the street, chased by a brisk fall breeze, and groups of people strolled by — churchgoers, joggers, and neighbors — all soaking in the last remnants of Indian summer.

Leah sat back in her chair and poured cream in her coffee. An amused smile played at the corners of her mouth. "About this land donation, Po — don't you wonder what Owen is saying about it all, wherever he is?"

"I suspect he's doing a bit of groaning right now."

"I know the church is important to Mary, but I don't think Owen ever set foot in that church, do you? As far as I know, he spent nearly every Sunday out on the golf course."

"He certainly wasn't religious in the same way Mary is," Po said. "Well, who knows. Maybe he'd consider this a good thing. He could contribute land, if not his presence, to the church."

"Po, you have this wonderful way of putting a good spin on everything. It's one of the reasons I love you so. But you and I both know that Owen loved that farm passionately. I could imagine him someday turning it into a nature sanctuary or an arboretum — a place where people nurtured their spirits privately, maybe . . . "

"A nature sanctuary with a putting green tucked away somewhere."

"Exactly."

"But apparently the Reverend had other things in mind. And I don't think Mary liked the farm particularly, so maybe this is the best thing to do. I'm sure it will be well-used, whatever Reverend Gottrey does with it."

Po scraped up the remaining eggs from her plate. Flakes of tarragon fell from her fork. "Marla has outdone herself today.

This is a great combination."

"It's a good thing we only do this once a week, Po," Leah murmured. "It takes me a week of running to work it off." She drained her orange juice, her eyes drifting to the moving figures outside the window. Suddenly she stopped, her glass in midair. "Po, look — " She pointed out the window.

Mary Hill walked slowly along the sidewalk. Her eyes downcast and her face the chalky color of the sidewalk. As she neared the café window, they saw the tears on her face, rolling down her cheeks and onto the collar of her suit. In her hand she clutched a piece of paper.

Po's heart lurched at the sight of the grieving widow. But before she could rise from her chair to comfort her, Mary turned down the narrow alley between Daisy's flower shop and the Brew and Brie and disappeared from sight. Po leaned from her chair and looked down the street in the opposite direction, half-expecting to see someone following her.

The street was empty.

♦

Chain   Links

Monday night quilting at Selma's shop was strictly a hit-or-miss gathering. Someone would drop by the store for needles or thread — or to ask Susan or Selma how to make the corners on a quilt binding come out square. And before long, there'd be three or four Bees sitting around the table drinking cups of Marla's coffee or diet soda and pulling squares of fabric from their bags. Lately the group was gathering with increased frequency, Po noticed, and it wasn't unusual for the whole group to gather — unofficially — beneath the skylight in Selma's back room. Usually they'd talk about books and movies and family news, new restaurants in town or who was running for the school board.

Tonight, however, they had more urgent things on their minds.

Phoebe and Kate walked in together, right after Po. Eleanor and Leah were already busy ironing the seams on several squares of stitched fabric. Kate hung her jacket on a hook near the back door and sat down at the table.

"Well, Po," she said, resting her elbows on the table, "It seems you were right."

Po looked up from the rich purple and gold print that would form the corners of her star. She pulled her glasses down to the tip of her nose. "If only I had a tape recorder," she said to Kate.

"Oh shush, Po — you know I almost always think you're right. But this time, you truly are." The tone in her voice was one of concern, though, rather than congratulations.

Selma was standing at the end of the table. "Kate, spill the beans before a customer comes in and I have to leave."

"The murder suspect was released. He wasn't the man who murdered Owen Hill. It was just like Po said."

Maggie and Susan came in from the front of the store. Susan was carrying a stack of calico-printed fabrics. "What did you say, Kate?" she asked.

"The man that they had in jail for Owen's murder," Phoebe answered for Kate. "That truck driver from Oklahoma — he didn't break in Selma's shop, and he didn't kill Owen Hill. For once, Marla had her facts straight."

"Well, I'll be," Eleanor said. The others were silent, absorbing the information. Susan sat down at the end of the table and fingered the stack of material. She looked at Kate and Phoebe intently. "How do you know this?"

"P.J. called me tonight as I was leaving to meet Phoebe," Kate said. "He was going to stop by the store himself, but things were crazy at the station. He wanted us . . ." — she looked over her shoulder at Selma — " . . . especially you, Selma, to know. Apparently the man was telling the truth — he found the watch and the wallet in a trash container at that truck plaza on the west side of town."

"How do they know he's telling the truth?" Susan asked.

"A couple of things — for one, he was nowhere near here the night Owen was killed. At first he didn't reveal his alibi, P.J. said, but he finally admitted that he was at that huge Rip Griffith truck stop in Limon on the night Owen was killed, halfway or more to Denver. Seems he has a girlfriend there. And a wife in Tulsa. That's why he was reluctant to mention it."

"But a murder charge trumped the wife finding out," Eleanor said. She was sitting quietly at one end of the table, piecing the tiny nine patches she was making for the center of her squares.

Kate continued. "Yes, it seems so. But there was more. A waitress at the truck plaza here in Crestwood saw the man going through the trash when she was out having a cigarette break. She remembered him because he was such a flirt. And right after he found the watch and wallet, he came into the restaurant, ordered a Kansas City Strip dinner, and left her a fifty dollar tip."

"Paid for by Owen Hill's credit card," Phoebe said.

"That's right. Apparently the police had their doubts all along — the whole thing didn't quite connect. But, as P.J. said, the town wants closure on this — there's an urgency to settle it. And there was circumstantial evidence — the watch and the credit card."

"What are the police going to do now?" Susan asked.

Po noticed the pillows beneath Susan's eyes and the fear in her voice. But who could blame her? A shadow of fear hovered over all the shop owners.

Kate poured herself a cup of coffee. "P.J. said the police are still saying it was a random robbery, but by this time the person is probably hundreds of miles away. It was unfortunate they picked up the wrong man, because timing is so important in cases like this."

"Is P.J. buying the robbery theory?" Po said.

The way Po said "P.J." made Kate's cheeks turn pink. "I don't know," she answered quickly.

"So that's it?" Selma said.

"I guess so, Selma. At least for now. It's going to be hard on Mary to have this all talked about again, but P.J. said people just have to move on."

"Move on?" Susan said. Her face was pale. She rose from the table and carried the stack of fabric into the other room.

"Is Susan all right?" Po asked.

"She's as concerned about me as anything," Selma said. "We spent some time on the books this weekend, and things aren't looking good. And having a man murdered on your doorstep doesn't do a lot for business. People come and gawk, but they aren't looking at fabric, I'm afraid."

Selma wrapped her fingers around the back of a chair.

"I don't know, Po. Sometimes I get so tired. Ever since Owen's murder, there has been a lot of tension among the shop owners. People didn't always like Owen because he took a hard stand on things — and his vote often determined what we did or didn't do. But he also had a stabilizing influence. And now others are trying to step into his shoes."

"How so?"

"Well, take Jess and Ambrose, for example. They're back on the brick sidewalk kick. It isn't just the cost of the sidewalks, but people trip on bricks, so insurance goes up, and they're harder to keep clear, so snow removal costs more. It's all a vicious circle. But now they're back at it again, campaigning among the other owners, having little private meetings."

"Won't it be more expensive for them, too?" Phoebe asked.

"Not so much. They have that narrow little store, so their fees aren't what mine are."

"I love their little store," Eleanor interjected as Maggie rethreaded the machine — she'd had to rewind the bobbin and, of course, it ran out halfway through a seam. "But I have noticed they're a little persnickety about things."

"They're determined to dictate taste for all the Elderberry shops, I fear," Selma said. "And though they don't actually say as much, I think a fabric shop is on the fringes of good taste, in their book. Not 'arty' enough."

"Selma, that's ridiculous," Eleanor said. Her voice was firm. "If these amazing quilts aren't works of art, nothing is."

"We may as well be weaving potholders," Selma said. "They view us as 'crafty.' They'd much rather have a fine china shop here, or yet another gallery of some sort. On some things, Owen was able to rein them in. Ambrose and Jess were afraid of him, I think." Her voice dropped off.

"They're just two people, Selma," Maggie said quietly.

"That's right. That's what I keep telling myself. Though one of them seems to have taken up permanent residence in Gus's bookstore, always trying to get his ear. It's just politics. It will be okay — I'm going to see if Susan needs help up front." She walked resolutely out of the room.

"It's awful that Selma has all this trouble on top of everything else," Phoebe said.

"I wonder how Mary feels about all this."

Po knew the answer to that. "Mary wants the new sidewalk."

"Well, ladies, we need to put our heads together and help Selma," Eleanor said.

Phoebe lifted her fabric square into the air. "For starters, we can make this quilt an unquestionable work of art. People will come from near and far to see it."

"Even from New York!" Maggie said.

For the next hour, Phoebe regaled them with stories of her energetic twins and the efficient way they had rearranged her house. "Nothing will ever be the same — and I love it!" She glanced at her watch. "Yikes, I promised to help Jimmy with the babies' baths tonight. So long, lovelies."

Phoebe's departure set the others in motion, sweeping up scraps and packing tote bags and satchels with fabric. Po packed up her bag and wandered into the front of the store. Kate had offered her a ride, but she wanted to check out some new fabrics Selma said had arrived that morning. She needed something subtle for the diamond she was piecing in the center of her star.

She wandered slowly past rows and rows, crowded with bolts of fabric. Selma's was like Gus's bookstore. Po could wander for hours, looking, reading, smelling. In times of stress, she found the soft fabric and rainbow of colors comforting. She looked up when she heard Selma shutting down the computer.

"Selma, am I keeping you from closing?"

"Nope. Take your time. Max is coming over to talk to me about something. Something about the corporation, he says."

"That's ominous."

"No. Max is a worrywart. And with Owen gone, he's taken on all these group disagreements himself. As our lawyer, he is determined to make the group work better together. Told me he wants to make sure Owen's work doesn't go unfinished, whatever the heck that means."

"Hmmm." Po picked up a crisp deep purple print. The pinpoints of pattern were barely visible, giving the fabric texture, without being busy. "Well, it's good you have someone like Max. He's sensible."

But Selma had gone into the backroom to lock the door and windows, and Po decided it was time to leave. She'd come back for the fabric tomorrow.

Max Elliot met her at the door.

"Good evening, Max," Po said pleasantly. Po had known Max for years. They'd been on a half dozen boards together and always enjoyed one another's company. Though they had different friends, they had skied together at Owen's farm several times. Po liked the pleasant-faced lawyer, and she admired the fact that he had resisted the lure of corporate law to keep his small office on Elderberry Road. Max handled everything from neighborhood feuds to estate planning to divorce, and always with a fair, kind hand. He had also been Owen Hill's closest friend, a fact Po could see etched into the deepening lines on his face.

"Hello, Po." Max held the door open for her. "Is Selma still around?"

Po nodded. "Yes. She's expecting you." Po started to walk on, then stopped briefly and turned around and called his name.

Max turned.

"I never got a chance to tell you, but please know how sorry I am about Owen. I know his death is an enormous loss to you."

Max offered a slight, sad smile. "Owen was the best sort of friend," he said quietly. "And I'll be relieved when this whole mess is settled and we can mourn him in peace."

"I guess you've heard that the wrong person was arrested."

For a time Max stood silent, looking at Po, but without seeing her. Po thought he was seeing something else, perhaps far away. Finally, he spoke. "Yes, I heard that."

"The police seem stymied." Po felt like she was rattling on, but Max seemed to have drifted off into a totally other place, and she wasn't sure how to end the conversation comfortably. "I guess what we need to do now is to somehow put this behind us." Po knew the words sounded hollow. But for once in her life she was at a loss for words. "We may never have a satisfying conclusion."

Max's eyes shifted, then came back to settle on Po. He was back from wherever he'd been, Po thought, but had brought something horrible with him.

"Po," he said forcefully — the power in his voice capturing Po's full attention. Max fixed her with a stare that made Po wish she had slipped out the back door and scooted on home, as had been her original plan.

Without averting his gaze for a second, Max reached out and took her arm. "Po, you are wrong about that. We are a long, long way from putting this behind us."

His grip was so tight that when he lifted his hand, small white ovals remained on Po's skin.

The usually mild-mannered man took a step back then, as if startled by his own intensity. His lips lifted in an attempt to smile but all Po saw was an enormous sadness. "I'm sorry, Po. It's a difficult time, is all." He slipped his hands into the pockets of his gray slacks, shook his head in apology. "And you're probably right that this won't be brought to a satisfying conclusion. Such ugly things never are. But it will be brought to some conclusion, with as few casualties as possible, one can hope."

Had he been born in an earlier time, Po thought, he would have tipped his hat at that moment and bowed slightly, then gallantly disappeared. Instead he simply nodded sadly and pushed his way through the heavy door of the quilt store.

Po watched him through the window until he disappeared behind a row of fabric. She wanted to follow him and make him explain himself. But of course she wouldn't.

Instead, she turned and walked toward the crescent moon that nearly touched the roofs of the Elderberry shops, her heart burdened by that awful sixth sense — that horrible, inexplicable foreboding.

CHAPTER 12

Storm at Sea

Po showered and slipped into a pair of jeans, pulled on her tennis shoes and a bright yellow sweatshirt, and headed for the kitchen and a cup of wake-up coffee. Hoover lumbered along behind her. After neglecting her book severely for over a week, she was determined to make some progress this morning.

She loved writing about these amazing women. With reluctance, she had finally finished the section on the Civil War and closed the chapter on the Underground Railroad and brave, young women like Elizabeth Keckley, a slave who had bought her freedom and become an amazing quilter. She took her young son and went to quilt for Mary Todd Lincoln, consoling the widow after her husband's tragic murder.

Po poured cold water into the coffee carafe and thought about the irony. While she was writing about one Mary coping with a murdered husband, another Mary, so close to Po's own life, was suffering the same.

Today she would move on to the suffrage movement and a young woman named Abigail Dunaway who migrated with her family to a new life in Oregon. Abigail began to quilt out of necessity — to provide warmth along the cold journey. And when forced to support her family, she did it the only way she knew how, by quilting.

Po opened the refrigerator and rummaged around for a bag of coffee beans. She thought about the impact the suffrage movement had on women. The leaders cried out for women to cast aside their sewing — a sign of subservience, some thought — and join the marches. And Abigail Dunaway did, marching and speaking and organizing masses of women to fight for their rights.

The attitude reminded Po briefly of the perception of some of the shop owners who thought a quilt shop unworthy of their block.

Po found it fascinating that something so intricate and amazing as the creation of a quilt could have been considered a lowly task and frowned upon so fiercely by women seeking rights to a bigger, more equal world. Of all the women she knew in the small town of Crestwood, the Queen Bees were among the most informed, self-contained, and the most comfortable in their own boots. And as for art — goodness, who could hold a candle to Susan's fine eye for color or Leah's amazing sense of space and shape?

What would she have done, living a century and a half ago? Po wondered. She put down her notes and set her glasses on the desktop. Probably what Abigail Dunaway did — yes, she might abandon her craft to speak her beliefs, to effect change. But wasn't it a good turn of history that crafts and art and liberated women could all live in the same room? And quilts were now displayed in the Smithsonian, in art galleries everywhere. It was a shame, she thought, closing the refrigerator door, that the Elderberry shop owners weren't so enlightened. Perhaps the Queen Bees could teach them a thing or two.

Po checked the cupboard shelf and sighed. No coffee anywhere. Beside the back door, Hoover greedily wolfed down his breakfast. He looked up at her, and she laughed. "No sweet pup, I won't eat yours."

But writing without coffee and something in her stomach besides vitamins wasn't going to happen, even about something as intriguing as the suffragettes. She'd go to plan "B."

In short order Po had filled her worn backpack with pencils, a pad of paper and her laptop computer. She would head for Elderberry Road, grab a cup of coffee at Marla's, and settle into a quiet corner in The Elderberry Bookstore. No ringing phone, no unexpected visitors, and the short walk would wake her up.

Gus's bookstore was never empty — even on a lazy weekday morning. There were the regulars — self-employed writers like herself, retired folks, and moms with small children

 115

who never missed story hour. And students liked to slip into cozy corners to study or write papers. Gus accommodated his clientele well, placing stuffed chairs and small tables throughout the well-stocked store — crammed on the first floor with new books, and on the lower level with thousands of used volumes. Po loved the comfortable old smells and streaks of dusty sunlight that slipped through the racks. So far Gus's store had held its own against the big chains and she suspected it would continue. They were a loyal crowd.

"Po Paltrow," Gus Schuette bellowed as she walked through the door. "What a welcome sight for these tired eyes. And just the person I need to see."

"And why's that, Gus?" Po continued toward the back of the store and her favorite niche, smack dab between the reference books and mysteries. She liked Gus, but knew firsthand how long conversations with him could be if there was something on his mind — and sometimes even if there wasn't. She settled into a red velvet chair and pulled her laptop out of the bag, positioning it on her knees.

Gus grabbed a straight-backed chair from a nearby table, dragged it over in front of Po and straddled it from behind, his arms dangling over the back of the chair. "It's this damn murder business, Po," he said. "How's Selma doing?"

"Selma?" Po pulled her glasses from her pocket and put them on. "Why do you ask?"

"You know — the talk. That she and Owen had an argument that night — a real doozy."

"From what I hear, you shop owners have perfected the fine art of arguing."

"Come on, Po, you know what I mean. Jesse and Ambrose

said they left the two of them going at it like a couple of mean roosters that night." Gus scratched his chin and pulled his thick brows together.

"Gus, what are you saying?"

"Oh, heck, Po, I don't know. But all this gossip, folks wondering why someone would come into a quilt store if he was looking for something to steal. Seems to be a lot more questions than answers, and it's not like it used to be around here. I wish they'd catch the guy."

"That may not happen."

Gus continued as if Po hadn't spoken. "Or maybe Jesse and Ambrose are right — maybe it's time for Selma to close that store. We could put in another gallery or something and start clean."

Po lifted her glasses to the top of her head and stared at Gus. She leaned forward in the chair. "Gus Schuette, what are you talking about? Start clean? And what makes a gallery cleaner than a quilt shop — or a bookstore, for that matter!"

"Oh, don't get your undies bunched, Po. It just feels tainted, that's all. That's what people are saying. There's this ugly shadow over the neighborhood. Maybe if someone took over that corner property, renovated it, fixed it up nice, we could forget about it and move on."

"Gus, I'm ashamed to hear you talk like that. You've known Selma all your life. How can you be so disloyal?"

Gus chewed on her words for a minute before answering. Then he lifted one leg across the chair and stood. "I guess maybe it does sound disloyal. But I know that my after-dark business isn't what it used to be. And Ambrose and Jesse said their wine bar clientele is dropping off, too. People seem nervous."

Po's heart sank. This kind of sentiment was bound to hurt Selma.

Gus looked over to the main desk near the door. He frowned. "There's Max Elliot, probably wanting to have another meeting with the owners. He's become a pain in the you-know-what."

Po looked across the store and saw Max talking to a customer. He had seemed so worried the day before. She'd asked Selma about his visit later, but Selma had shrugged it off. Said Max was a decent man, was all. He wanted to help everyone — her, Mary, Ambrose. Most of all he wanted things done right and fairly.

"Max Elliot is mad as a wet hen at all of us," Gus said. "He wants to check this, check that, make sure everyone's audits are done. Heck, we don't have time for all that. He and Owen had taken on some kind of a crusade around here. But who knows — maybe Max will move on now. He was only around because he was Owen's best friend — we could use some fresh lawyer blood."

At that moment, Ambrose Sweet appeared around the edge of the bookshelf, his arms heavy with books. "Well, hello, you two. Having a little tete-á-tete back here in the thick of the mysteries? And talking about blood? Oh, my." He clicked his tongue against his teeth and shook one long finger at them from beneath the pile of books.

"Hi Ambrose," Gus said as he swung the chair back into place. "Looks like you're set for some heavy reading."

Po noticed the titles of the top two books: *Legal Loopholes for the Small Shop Owner, Tax Breaks Beyond the Norm.*

Ambrose followed her gaze. "Owning a store is more than knowing where to get the finest cabernet at the best price," he said. Then he winked at Po as if the two of them shared a profound secret.

Po found the gesture irritating. "Doesn't Max handle that sort of thing for you?" she asked.

"Oh, Max? Yes, Max is involved in everything, thanks to Sir Owen Hill." Ambrose rolled his eyes, then leaned forward from his slender waist and said in a hushed tone, "God helps those who help themselves, Po."

Ambrose spotted a book on the shelf behind Po that interested him, and managed to pull it out of its tight space and wedge it beneath his arm. With a small wave, he strode off toward the front of the store.

"Curious fellow," Gus said as Ambrose Sweet walked off. "But he and Jesse are running a mighty fine shop. Carry only the best liquors, wine, cheese, glassware. Great for the neighborhood."

With that, Gus, too, strode off. Po watched the two men move toward the curved oak counter near the store's entrance. Curious wasn't the word Po would have picked for Ambrose, though he was a bit of that, she supposed. She admired his store, loved the wines and cheeses he carried, but she was never quite comfortable in his presence. His partner Jesse was much easier to be around — a sweet, handsome man with a wry wit, he was usually the one she turned to with advice on the wine and cheese baskets she sent off to her children for special occasions.

A small slip of paper caught her eye as she tried to shift her concentration back to suffragettes and quilts and the march of brave women through time. Holding her computer firm with one hand, she leaned over and picked it up. It must have dropped from one of Ambrose's books, she thought. Probably a makeshift bookmark. Sometimes people used Gus's store more like a library than a place to purchase books, and Po herself had found signs of others in books she'd purchased — a stray receipt, a grocery list on the back of an envelope. The words scribbled across the piece of notepaper in her hand were large and uneven, but the first one caught her eye: "Parker."

And beneath it in a bulleted list were the others: "Sidewalk. New Tenants. Gallery. French restaurant. Out with the old, in with the new," was scribbled across the bottom in smaller script.

Po scrunched up the note in her hand and shook her head. When would all this stop, she wondered, and quietly packed up her computer. Clearly she was to get no writing done this morning.

CHAPTER 13

Light and Dark

Although Thursday wasn't a usual gathering night for the Queen Bees, Phoebe sent an e-mail to everyone Wednesday night. In it, she suggested they all gather the next night to put in extra work on Selma's quilt. She had a surprise for everyone, she said, and if that wasn't enough incentive, perhaps Kate's shrimp and feta cheese dish would do it.

Thinking about Phoebe's e-mail made Po smile. She had run into Phoebe at Dillon's Market over on River Road after leaving the Elderberry Bookstore. Phoebe was maneuvering a clumsy grocery cart down the cereal aisle with Jude and Emma strapped into the cart's safety seats. While Phoebe grabbed cereal and apples and bags of pasta from the shelves, the twins, their round faces bright, tossed whatever was within reach into the air and clapped happily when something landed on the floor.

Po scooped up Emma first and hugged her close, and then Jude, marveling over how big the twins had gotten. She drank in their unfettered smiles, their sweet giggles. And in between, she shared with Phoebe the dour talk around Elderberry Road, and especially about Selma's shop.

Po knew the e-mail had been prompted more by that conversation than concern for the quilt's progress. Phoebe thought it would cheer up Selma, bless her crazy little soul.

Po stopped at Jesse and Ambrose's for a couple bottles of wine and arrived at Selma's just as Kate brought her old green Jeep to a screeching halt outside the alley door. The evening had turned chilly and it was already dark. Po pulled up the collar of her fleece jacket and waited at the back door for Kate. "I can smell that casserole all the way out here," she said as Kate opened the car door.

"And you're just in time to carry one in." Kate handed one glass dish to Po, then lifted the other and shut the door with her elbow. "Thanks, Po. How's the book coming?"

"Slowly. Too many distractions. But being with the Queen Bees is always inspiring, so tomorrow I will write like a wild woman."

Kate laughed. "You write so beautifully, Po. You could write about doing your laundry and I'd read it with great pleasure."

"Spoken like a true goddaughter." Po smiled, pleased. She wanted to ask Kate about P.J. but held her silence. She had called Kate the night before and hadn't gotten an answer, but later Leah mentioned that she'd run into Kate and P.J. at a film festival on campus. "Looked chummy," Leah had said.

"I've seen P.J. a couple of times this week, Po," Kate said. "I like him — even more than I did in high school."

Po's look of surprise made Kate laugh. "Didn't know I could read your mind, Po?" She balanced the casserole on her hip and planted a kiss on Po's cheek. "There. That's for loving me."

Po fought off an irresistible urge to shed a tear — for Kate's affection, for Selma's troubles. For this circle of women who stopped their lives to come together over shrimp and feta cheese casserole to make a friend feel better.

"Stop it, you," she said aloud, her husky voice a level lower than usual. "Let's get this food inside before we drop it."

"Which, as you well know, is a distinct possibility." Kate grinned and moved toward the door.

A large, hefty figure emerged from the shadowy path between Selma's store and the empty shop next door.

"Ladies, let me —" a thick, gravely voice said.

Kate jumped. The casserole slipped in her hands.

The unshaven security guard shuffled over to the door and held it open. Kate regained control of the glass dish and moved quickly inside, followed by Po. The man nodded his head at Po as she passed. The smell of liquor filled the air between them.

"Thank you," Po said as she passed, then hurried after Kate. She turned to be sure he'd closed the door tightly and watched him walk away, swinging a flashlight and mumbling at the moon. Strange man, she thought to herself. And he certainly didn't make her feel secure.

"He scares me," Kate whispered. "He lurks," she added.

Po nodded. "Selma says he's harmless, but I wouldn't turn my back on him ..."

". . . In a dark alley," Kate added, glancing out the window.

"Hi there, ladies," Maggie called out and Kate and Po turned their attention to the bustling, welcoming scene spread out in front of them.

Maggie had plugged in a hot tray to keep Kate's casseroles warm and had wrapped a French baguette in a plaid towel. Eleanor was tossing a huge salad on a small round table on the far side of the room, while Leah arranged the napkins and plastic cups on the side shelf. And in the center of the sewing table, filled with cattails, partridge peas, and crimson and gold mums, was Maggie's latest acquisition — a clay vase molded in the shape of a voluptuous woman with a secret smile on her face.

"She's beautiful, Maggie," Kate murmured. "What do you suppose she's thinking?"

"Ah, that's for her to know, for us to imagine," Po said wisely. "But one can imagine . . ."

"One of my clients made her. I think I'll soon have the finest collection of fat lady art in the world. Or at least in Kansas. I call her Anastasia."

"I think this is my favorite so far," Po said, sliding her fingers over the smooth curves of the lovely figure. "Though I love the painting of the ladies at the beach."

"How nice that clients bring you gifts," Kate said.

"We've been crazy busy at the clinic, and I've stayed late to accommodate some people. Sometimes they say thanks with a gift. It sure isn't necessary — but I love this one."

"Why so busy?" Kate asked. "Fleas should be behind us, right?" She picked a cucumber out of the salad and nibbled on it.

"This isn't about fleas. People are bringing in new pets for their shots and checkups — a normal thing to do — but they're coming in droves and they're not bringing in puppies. It's been a week of BIG dogs — Great Danes, Dobermans, German shepherds."

"I know what triggered that — an article in that poor excuse Crestwood calls a paper," Eleanor said. "It's worse than the *National Enquirer* if you ask me. The foolish reporter suggested that with all the crime in Crestwood, people should think about ways to safeguard their homes. Burglar alarms, lights all over your house so you can't sleep, and even hiring your own private security guard. Buying an enormous guard dog took up a whole column. They listed everything but duct tape."

Leah laughed. "'All the crime in Crestwood.' That sounds like a murder a month here."

"Sells papers, I guess," said Maggie. "It may be silly, but people working at the animal shelter are happy. Lots of dogs that were considered tough placements — the ones that aren't cute, fluffy puppies — have been adopted."

Susan and Selma walked in from the front of the store. The shop was closed on Thursday nights and the two had just finished closing up the day's business.

"I smell a feast," Selma said. She pulled the foil from a

corner of Kate's casserole and closed her eyes, drinking in the mushroom and wine-scented steam. "This is just what I needed tonight. I have to leave for a bit but save me some, you hear?" She wagged a finger at Kate. "This stuff is sinful — and I need sin tonight."

"Bad day, Selma?" Kate asked.

"Bad week. But it will get better."

"What's going on tonight, Selma?" Po asked. "I thought you were free."

"Max Elliott came by a little bit ago and had his dander up about something. He's insisting all the shop owners meet tonight." She sighed.

"For what?" Po noticed that the lines in Selma's face had deepened over the past few days. She looked smaller and weighted down, as if the force of gravity had suddenly increased.

Selma shrugged. "I think Max is trying to make sense of all the notes Owen left him about the corporation. Something about corporation books not balancing, needing audits, all that sort of mumble jumble. But he's being so damn mysterious about it all. I say just out with it, whatever the heck it is, then fix it. And then move on. Anything but a meeting. But he insisted. Said it wouldn't take long."

"Where are you meeting?" Eleanor asked. "Do you need this room?"

"No. Mary volunteered Windsor House. Max had something to do first — something he couldn't get out of, he said. He'll be there at eight, though, and he practically ordered me not to be late."

"Windsor House was dark when I walked by," Leah said.

"But Mary will open up for the meeting. She has a nice back room, just like this. By the way . . ." Selma looked around the room and frowned. "It's far too quiet in here. Where's Phoebe?"

"Ta-da!" As if on cue, Phoebe swept through the back door of the store.

"Phoebe!" Seven voices rose like steam from hot coffee and collided directly over Phoebe Mellon's newly shorn head.

"Like it?" Phoebe asked, pirouetting around the quilting table like a ballet dancer.

"It's . . . short," Leah said.

"Good gracious," Eleanor said.

"Hair today, gone tomorrow," Phoebe said, her eyes shining.

"Phoebe, you rascal," Selma uttered, her fingers pressed to her lips.

Kate walked over to Phoebe and looked at the shining platinum globe from all angles. "Pheebs," she declared, "I like it! It's cool — very chic."

Maggie started to laugh. "Phoebe, you're the best. It's great. You go, girl!"

Phoebe giggled. "Yeah, that's what Jimmy said his parents would say — you go, girl."

"However did you do that?" Eleanor said. She touched her own cap of gray hair as if to guard it.

"It's the miracle of the Flow bee, Eleanor. It's the greatest. I'm going to do Jimmy's. And when you're ready for a cut, I'm your person." She turned toward Po. "Well, bee keeper — what do you think?"

"I think you're handsome, Phoebe, and you'll probably

start a trend. But in the meantime, you might consider stocking up on wool caps for the winter. Perhaps El would knit you one." Truth be known, she thought Phoebe looked beautiful. Her hair was a one-inch cap of sunshine.

"Well, I'd just had it with running out of the house with wet hair, never having time to dry it, and always fearful that the twins would grab the hairdryer. One night I couldn't sleep so I turned on the TV and saw this amazing gadget advertised — you hook it up to your vacuum cleaner."

"Phoebe!" Kate yelped. She touched her thick head of hair and imagined it being attached to a vacuum hose.

"No, Kate, it's great. Honest. It sucks your hair up and you just slice it all off at whatever length you want." She grinned, twirled around again and ran her fingers through her glimmering Joan of Arc do. "Now all the time I used to spend untangling my hair, I get to spend with my beautiful babies. How good is that? I love it." She patted the side of her head softly. "And Jude and Emma love it, too."

"And Jimmy?"

"Jimmy — hmmm, well, Jimmy will adjust. I think he's a little nervous about the Harvest Ball at his folks' club in a couple weeks — but it will be fine."

"You look just like Mary Martin in that old Peter Pan production," Eleanor said. "And if those Mellons say a single word, I'll clobber them with my cane. Stuffy old busybodies."

Phoebe beamed.

Selma glanced at her watch, then walked over and gave Phoebe a gruff hug. "Sweetie, you're a crazy girl. Keep it that way — you bring sunshine into our lives." She grabbed a thick gray sweater from the coat rack and shoved her arms into the sleeves. "I'm five minutes late — Max will be having a holy fit." She took a deep breath and rested one hand on the door. "If I'm not back in half an hour, girls, send out the dogs." Selma pushed open the back door and disappeared down the dark alley.

"Selma looked worried to me," Kate said.

"Maybe a little." Maggie agreed.

Susan sat silently at the table, staring through the window at Selma's retreating figure.

"Susan?" Kate asked.

"Susan — are you all right?" Po asked. She walked over and sat down beside her. Susan had her hair pulled back in a ponytail. She wore little makeup. Dressed in jeans and a faded Canterbury College sweatshirt, she looked more like a teenager than a thirty-eight-year-old woman. There was a dramatic beauty about her made even more pronounced by the emotion in her eyes.

Susan offered a slight smile. "Late nights, that's all. I have a couple papers due at school. Mid-term time . . ."

"I know that feeling, Susan," Kate said, sitting down on her other side.

"Well, too much work isn't good for anyone," Po said. "We need to consider that February quilt retreat down in Florida that Selma told us about last month. Be good for all of us." Po reached for her bag and pulled out her glasses and several strips of the deep rose fabric she had finally chosen for the center of her stars.

"That's a terrific idea, Po. Maybe I'd finally learn how to stitch those blasted curves," Eleanor said. "Besides, leaving Kansas in February is a good and wise thing to do. Count me

Light and Dark

in — and we can all stay in my home down there if you'd like."

Phoebe walked over and planted a kiss on Eleanor's cheek. "You are a cool lady, Eleanor. You scared me a little when I first joined this group, but you've grown on me like a nice cashmere sweater."

Eleanor's laughter was deep and loose — in the way of people who had seen a lot, lived fully, and chose freely what to let in or keep out of their lives. She tilted her head back and looked at Phoebe. "Well, missy, I wasn't so sure of you, either — at least not for a minute or two. You were one sassy lass. But then you whipped out that needle of yours and stitched up those blocks for the Jacob's Ladder quilt we made for the women's shelter, and I thought, 'now she can't be all bad, and she's kind of cute, with all those dangly little earrings hanging from her ears — reminds me a little of me at that age.'"

Phoebe pushed Eleanor's hair away from her ear. "Eleanor Elizabeth Canterbury — oh my soul!"

Eleanor slapped Phoebe's hand away and her soft gray hair fall back over her ear. "You mind your manners, Phoebe Mellon, or I'll take you over my knee."

Phoebe was undeterred. "Eleanor's ear has three tiny holes in it — I saw it with my own eyes. Eleanor, you gypsy you." Phoebe put her hands on her hips, threw back her head and laughed.

A sudden, insistent rattle pulled everyone's attention to the back door.

"What's all the racket?" a man's voice asked. "I thought this was a serious group."

"Hey, P.J.," Phoebe said. "Come on in. You're just in time."

P.J. took one step inside the door and stopped. "Don't want to intrude."

"Well of course you do," Po laughed. "Get yourself in here and talk to us."

"I saw the lights, is all." P.J.'s head nearly touched the top of the doorframe. He walked over to the table and looked around at the piles of fabric. "I wanted to be sure you ladies were okay."

"P.J., you came in here because you smelled food, 'fess up," Maggie said.

"Well —" He tried to look sheepish. "I did hear a rumor that there might be a feast back here. Heard some talk of a shrimp casserole. And I haven't eaten for — well, days, I think." He looked sideways at Kate.

Kate laughed. "Flanigan, you're hopeless," she said.

Po noticed the slight blush that colored Kate's cheeks. It was very becoming on her.

P.J. walked across the room. "Hey, Phoebe Mellon," he said, spotting the small figure sitting next to Eleanor. "Nice hair, munchkin."

Phoebe touched it with the tips of her fingers. "I like it, too."

"How's Jimmy doing? Saw him over at the Court House the other day working his magic at a trial."

"He's doing fine. Working hard to sort out the bad apples from the good and protect the innocent," Phoebe laughed. "Just like you, P.J."

"We try, Phoebe."

A series of gongs from the grandfather clock in the front of the store broke through the chatter and Po glanced down at her watch. "Selma should be here in a second, and we'll dish it all up. Kate made enough for a marching band, P.J. You're welcome to feed that fine frame of yours."

"Well, now, Po, that's mighty nice of you." He tipped his head in her direction and a lock of brown hair fell across his forehead.

Po had forgotten just how engaging a grin P.J. Flanigan had — just like Pete Flanigan senior. It was as crooked as the streets in Crestwood — starting out in the right place and then spreading clear across that handsome face of his. She wondered if Kate noticed.

"There's Selma now," Kate said, pointing out the back window.

The back door flew open and Selma burst through, the edges of her long wooly sweater flapping against her hips. "Well, how's that for a wasted hour!" She shrugged out of the sweater and hung it back on the hook. "I think I'm ready for that wine now, thank you very much."

"What happened, Selma?" Po walked over to the sideboard and poured a glass of Ambrose's special cabernet. She handed it to Selma. "You look angry. Or worried. I can't tell which."

"What's the big dark secret Max had?" Phoebe asked.

Selma started to answer, then noticed P.J. standing behind Kate. Her face blanched. "P.J., what are you doing here? Is everything all right?"

"This is strictly social, Selma. I'm off duty."

"Well, maybe you better get on duty — seems Max Elliott has disappeared into the night. Either that, or he stood us all up. One worries me, one makes me furious. Which should I be?"

"Max didn't come?" Po's elegant brows lifted.

"Never showed." Selma took a sip of the wine and sighed. "And you could have cut the tension in that group with Susan's cake knife over there . . ." She nodded toward the double chocolate mousse cake Susan had contributed to the supper. "Tempers were high, let me tell you."

"Why's that?" Maggie asked. "It was just a meeting."

"No, no. Not just a meeting. Max had cloaked it in urgency and mystery. According to someone — maybe Daisy — Owen had instructed Max to clean things up, so to speak. Audit books. Check on our contractors — repairmen, roofers, maintenance folks. Thought there was some sneaky stuff going on. It all had some folks on edge."

"I don't get it," said Maggie.

"I'm not sure I do, either, Maggie. Owen seemed to think that favors were being done, people being hired who shouldn't have been. Who knows what he thought. I'm not sure I care."

She sat down at the end of the table.

Po shook her head. "It doesn't sound like Max Elliott not to show up, especially if he had things on his mind. Marla says she sets her clock by him coming in for coffee in the morning. Eight o'clock on the dot."

Selma nodded. "You're right. He's irritatingly punctual. But we called his house and Ambrose even went over to his office to check."

Kate spoke up. "Didn't you say he had something earlier, Selma? Maybe it just went late."

"We thought of that. But why didn't he call? He never lets that cell phone out of his sight, far as I can tell."

A soft ring broke into the conversation. P.J.'s hand went automatically to his shirt pocket. "Sorry, ladies," he said apologetically. He slipped the phone out, flipped open the lid and read the number across the screen. "I better take this."

P.J. moved into the front room to take his call.

Leah walked over to the sideboard and took the foil off Kate's casserole. "Lately Max looked like he was carrying the world on those slight shoulders of his," she said. "I saw him at a party the other night and he wasn't himself. He asked me about the quilting group, who was in it, that sort of thing, which I thought was odd. Wanted to know what nights we were here."

"I wonder if he just got sick of all these squabbles with the shop owners. Maybe he just threw in the towel and decided not to come," Selma said. "We can be an ornery group."

"You know he wouldn't do that, Selma," Susan said softly.

"Of course he wouldn't. It's just that mad is easier than worry these days. I don't want one more thing to worry about." She saw Kate look up and turned to follow her gaze.

P.J. stood in the archway, his phone still in his hand. His face was grave, the beguiling smile gone.

"P.J.," Kate said, "What's wrong?"

"Bad news, ladies," he said softly. "Max Elliot is in the hospital."

"What?" Selma's hands rose to her face.

"But, why would they call you, P.J.?" Kate's voice shook. She knew she wasn't going to like his answer, nor were any of the women in the small, cozy quilting room.

"Someone ran him down in the street," P.J. said simply. "And Max is hanging on by a thread."

He looked longingly at the casserole, then gave Kate a quick, discrete hug, and disappeared out the back door.

CHAPTER 14

Flock of Birds

Po slept fitfully that night. When the old mariner's clock in the study chimed six times, she gave up the fight and slipped out of bed. A quick shower and several long stretches — her torso dipping until her hands were flat on the floor — started her blood moving through her veins. She bent at the waist again, reached low and slowly raised her body up. Yes, she could face the day. She slipped into jeans and a turtleneck and headed for the kitchen, forking her fingers through her hair to untangle the loose, damp waves around her face.

In the hallway, she stumbled over a sleeping Hoover. The floppy mutt lifted his red head and licked her leg, then settled back down.

"Some guard dog, you are," Po grumbled affectionately. Hoover's tail flapped slowly in acknowledgement.

The phone rang as Po was pouring water into the carafe.

Six o'clock phone calls were never happy ones. Po closed her eyes, took a deep breath, and said hello.

"I'll be by in ten minutes," Kate said. "Is the coffee on?"

Po could hear echoing noises in the background and suspected Kate was on her cell phone. "Kate, where are you?"

"Running up from the river jogging path. I'm a few minutes from Elderberry Road. We'll be there before the banana bread is thawed." The phone went dead.

We? Po wondered, and took three mugs from the cupboard.

Ten minutes later, a sweaty, lanky Kate arrived at the back door. A well-worn Trolley Run tee shirt clung to her shoulders. Her high cheek bones and arms were glossy with moisture. Damp, auburn curls made paisley designs on her forehead.

"I couldn't sleep, Po," Kate said, heading for the refrigerator. "And if I couldn't, I knew you couldn't either." She bent over and rummaged through the refrigerator, found a bottle of water, and closed the door.

"About this we . . .," Po began, but before the words were out of her mouth, P.J. appeared at the door.

"She wouldn't wait for me, Po, wouldn't even pretend I was faster. What kind of woman is that?" P.J. stood in the back doorway with his hands on his hips, his chest moving in and out as he sucked in mouthfuls of air. His damp shorts clung to strong muscular legs, and Po wondered who was pretending for whom.

Po poured three mugs of coffee and set them on the long table. Early sunlight poured through the east windows, lighting the table and basking the kitchen in a deceptive calm.

"The news didn't hit the morning paper," P.J. began, settling into a kitchen chair. Po noticed that he spread a towel across the seat first to blot up his body's damp heat.

"No, I imagined it would be too late for the *Crestwood Courier*. Have you heard anything more, P.J.?"

"A little. Max was hit on West 2nd Street, over near that strip of supply stores on the west side of town. There's a little diner on the block, but not much else besides the warehouses. It's right before you get to the highway, about fifteen minutes from here in light traffic."

Po nodded. She knew the place. There was a garden supply store nearby that she often went to.

"Have they found out what he was doing there?" Kate asked. P.J. had called her late the night before, but with little information. He called, he said, to make sure all the Queen Bees got home okay. And to say goodnight. And he wondered if there was any shrimp casserole left.

P.J. shook his head in answer to her question. "Nope. It's pretty deserted around there at that time of night, except for the diner. His car was across the street, and from where he was hit and the angle of his arms and legs, it looks like that's where he was headed."

"How awful that the person didn't stop," Po said. The ping of the oven timer announced that her banana bread was

Flock of Birds

ready. She took it out and brought it back to the table with a bowl of sweet butter and strawberry jam.

"It's awful, Po, sure. But definitely understandable." P.J. helped himself to a thick slab of bread and slathered it with jam. "This is terrific, Po," he mumbled between bites.

"It's never understandable, or acceptable, P.J.," Po said. She frowned at him. "Why would anyone run away from an accident in which someone was hurt?"

"Because they didn't want to get caught, Po, that's why. And it wasn't an accident. Max Elliott was hit on purpose. Someone wanted to kill him, and damn near did."

CHAPTER 15

Snail's Trail

By Saturday, everyone in Crestwood, Kansas, knew about the hit-and-run attempt to kill Max Elliott. And according to the Saturday paper, it could still be a case of murder. Max Elliott was in a coma and his condition grave. The mood in the back of Selma's store when the Queen Bees began to gather was somber.

"It was an old pickup truck," Maggie said.

"And how many thousands of those will you find around here?" Eleanor asked.

"I've got one," Maggie raised her hand.

"Exactly," Kate said. "There are zillions. P.J. said it's going to take a stroke of luck to move this forward.

"But isn't there a witness?" Maggie asked.

"Yes, but he was loaded," Kate said. "An older man who had just come out of a bar around the corner and probably wouldn't have seen anything except the pick-up came out of nowhere and nearly ran him down. The guy fell back on the curb and sat up just in time to see the truck slam into Max. At first the guy thought the truck was stopping, an honest accident, but then it sped off."

Susan had walked in while they were talking and shivered as she heard the description. She ran her hands up and down her bare arms. "Max wouldn't hurt a flea. This is so awful."

Po watched the lines of worry and fear flit across Susan's face. For a minute, it looked like Susan was going to say something, but then her eyes blinked and she looked away.

"We need action." Phoebe had come in the front door and stood in the archway, hands on her hips.

"Phoebe, where are you going — a Harley rally?" Maggie asked.

Phoebe was dressed completely in black — tight jeans and turtleneck, a black cap that nearly covered her shorn hair, and high top tennis shoes. Po thought she looked like a little black cat.

"I think it's time we got organized," Phoebe said. "This is definitely too close to home. We need to get the person who did this and put an end to it all, once and for all. And if you believe there isn't a connection between what happened last night and Owen Hill's murder, then you don't watch enough 'Law and Order' reruns."

Kate nodded. "They're looking for a connection between the two; Phoebe's right."

"I can't imagine anyone in this whole world who would want to kill Owen and Max," Leah said. She'd already pieced all her stars and was cutting the pieces for the backing — one huge star that matched the smaller ones on the front.

"Poor Mary," Maggie said. "First her husband, then his best friend. I wonder how she's holding up."

"She looks frail," Eleanor said. "Instead of getting stronger, she's wilting like a pansy in July."

"I saw her and Max Thursday," Kate said. "They were outside Daisy's shop. I started to say hello, but Mary was very upset. Dear sweet Max had his arm around her, comforting her."

"I think her church has rallied around her, too," Po said. "I invited her to a couple of upcoming events, but the Reverend and his wife beat me to it. They've booked most of her evenings."

"Hah!" Eleanor snorted. "Of course they have. With Owen gone, they have direct access to the Hill fortune."

"Eleanor, that's harsh," Po said. "And Mary is a business woman. She's not about to give all her money away indiscriminately."

"Po, sometimes you're too blasted diplomatic for your own good. Face it, without Owen to temper the gifts to the church, Reverend Gottrey will take off like a racehorse, wooing Mary for all she's worth."

"Which is a lot," Po conceded. "But the donations are for a good cause, and it's Mary's money now to do with as she wishes."

"Reverend Gottrey made Mary an elder of the church last week. And the Hill name will be on so many plaques that they'll be able to build a barn out of them," Eleanor said.

Phoebe sided with her. "Eleanor, not only are you getting very good at sewing corners that meet in the right place, you're sensible. You may be on to something. It seems to me this investigation is moving at a snail's pace — they should have this man in jail by now, before someone else gets killed. Maybe we can help speed it up."

"I for one will do anything I can to help Selma," Maggie said. "If that means snooping around or gathering information, I'm in, but I refuse to wear a black cat suit."

"But Mags, you'd look so cute," Kate teased.

Maggie laughed and got up to press out her seams before sewing on the next piece.

Po stood at the end of the table and watched a dozen fingers pinning bright star points together, pressing seams, carefully lining up fabric on green cutting mats. Lips were pursed, eyes focused, and throughout it all, bits of conversation were woven into the process effortlessly.

She thought about what Phoebe said. Similar thoughts had spun around inside her head in the early hours of the morning when sleep had totally abandoned her. Who did this awful thing? And were they all in danger now — the quilters, the shopkeepers, neighbors? Their safe, small world had been disrupted. It was etched in the deep lines in Selma's face, the fear that Susan carried on her sleeve, the sleeplessness and suspicions. She could even detect it in the loose chatter of Maggie and Kate, who tried to be affirming and positive.

"We all need to be careful, that much is for sure," Po said, more to herself than to the group. If they could string some thoughts together that made sense and speed things up, what harm would be done? She walked over to the sideboard and poured herself a cup of coffee, her gaze shifting from the quilters to the alley outside the window. It was difficult to believe that it was two weeks ago today that she had stumbled upon Owen's body in that alley. Did someone surprise him? Or was it someone he knew?

Po turned away from the window. "I think we need to approach this like a new quilt," she said. "But we need to think outside the single squares and think about the bigger pattern."

Phoebe looked up, her eyes lit with excitement. "And just like we do with our pieces of fabric: We take the whole big piece and cut it into little pieces, then put it back together in lots of different ways."

"Okay, ladies," Eleanor said, her rotary cutter held high in the air, "let's cut!"

"—to the chase," Phoebe added.

In short order, the Queen Bees had gone over everything they knew, beginning with the night of Owen's murder and ending with Max's hit-and-run. How such momentous events — the shifting and changing forever of lives — could be packed into a brief summary was thought provoking to Po. She wanted to gather her three children close and embrace them tightly.

"All right," she said. "Where do we go from here? Any suggestions?"

"I think we should have little assignments," Phoebe said.

"We could do it loosely, maybe," Maggie said. "I'll listen carefully to what my clients say."

"And I can keep track of the college talk," Leah added.

"I seem to spend a great deal of time in these shops. I'll talk to Gus and Ambrose," Po said.

"And Daisy?" Leah asked, knowing approaching Daisy Sample could be dangerous to your health, if not done with great delicacy.

Po laughed. "Daisy doesn't frighten me. In fact, I kind of like her. She has chutzpah."

"And Kate, you keep close track of P.J.," Maggie said with a suggestive smile. "That way we get news from the horse's mouth."

"And Selma and Susan are here in the middle of the tempest," Kate said, ignoring Maggie's innuendoes. "So they can gather on-the-spot news."

"We keep our ears open, our eyes focused," Leah said, summing it up.

"Yes, that's it in a nutshell. So Bees," Phoebe said, rising from her chair and punching the air with her fists. "Let's sleuth!"

◆

C H A P T E R   1 6

S p i d e r   &   t h e   F l y

Po sat at her computer in the late-Saturday afternoon light, the stories of strong women parading across her mind like frames of a movie. She had run a half-dozen quick errands after leaving the quilting group, keeping her ears and eyes open as instructed, then headed home to get in a couple of hours at the computer, moving her book along to the next moment in history. She was going from one group of strong women to another, she thought, replaying the morning's quilting session in her mind. Each of the Queen Bees wanted so desperately to help bring order and peace back to Selma's life. The sleuthing may not amount to anything, but at least it made them all feel useful.

Po focused on the screen and began to read what she'd most recently written. Strong women everywhere, she thought. The writing had flowed and the stories seemed to pour out on top of one another. And tied into the story of each of these brave women was their passion for quilting and the fierce bonds they forged as they sat in soft, comfortable silence, creating designs that would be passed down for generations.

The stories were vital to Po — whether they were myths, as some thought, or not — and she cherished the idea of women hanging Jacob's Ladder quilts on clothes lines as a message to runaway slaves. The black square in the center said, "You're safe here — come in." She thought of women in wartime, left at home to work in factories, keeping their families safe and fed. They gathered scraps of firecracker red, strips of white and blue, and wove them into patriotic quilts that they raffled off to collect money for the war effort.

Po wrote for a while, until her shoulders began to sag and the small space in her lower back cried for movement. Hoover cried for movement, too, his patience as frayed as his floppy tail.

"Okay, pal," Po said. "It's almost dark, but let's go for a romp."

Wrapped in a fuzzy red jacket and pulling a cap over her ears, Po set out for the Elderberry shops. As long as she was out, she'd pick up some bread for tomorrow's supper, too, if

Marla had any left. The stores closed at six on Saturday nights, but the closing time wasn't written in stone. The hours became as unpredictable as the owners and she suspected she'd find something still open, even though the hour hand on the mantle clock had edged past six.

The decorative gaslights that lit Elderberry Road were already on by the time Hoover and Po turned down the street. The sky ahead of her still held a trace of sunlight, but behind it was already night. Though the air was still tinged with autumn, the winter smells were there, too. Po could feel them. And in her mind's eye she saw the diamond flakes drifting down silently around the gaslights, white piles forming on the heavy black bases. A scene straight out of Currier and Ives.

Just as she reached Marla's, the lights flickered, then went out. A faceless hand flipped the window sign to "Closed," and behind the thin curtain, Po could see Marla shuffling off toward the back of the bakery. No matter. She could pick up the bread tomorrow when she and Leah met for breakfast.

She and Hoover had the block to themselves and they walked on down the row of shops. As they passed the Flowers by Daisy shop, Po noticed that Daisy had increased her bed of plastic flowers — probably out of spite, she thought — and further down, Gus had a new display of books in the window. "Banned books," the sign read, and beneath it was a delightful display of some of Po's favorite masterpieces. She stopped and peered through the glass, reading each title carefully, catching herself tsking out loud now and then at such folly. *Catcher in the Rye, Gone with the Wind, The Twelfth Night, Tom Sawyer, The Origin of the*

Species. And, oh, my, one she hadn't known about before: a 1989 school ban on *Little Red Riding Hood.* Good for Gus. Raising awareness was never a bad thing. And it was certainly something they were all being called to do these recent days.

A shadow fell across the sidewalk behind her and she glanced back to see who was coming. It was Wesley Peet, swinging a lit flashlight, his gait unsteady. Hoover growled and his ears shot up.

Po grabbed his leash and whispered soothing, quieting words, her eyes not leaving the brawny shadow behind the flashlight. The light cast eerie, jagged streaks across the sidewalk.

Suddenly the beam of light changed direction. Instead of continuing on toward her, Wesley turned down the narrow alley between Daisy's and the Brew and Brie and disappeared.

Po wasn't even sure he had seen her. She shivered. Suddenly the night was darker, the air sharper, and winter seemed far closer than it had earlier in the day. She remembered what someone had said recently about Owen, that he was about to fire Wesley. At the time, it hadn't seemed important. Now, everything seemed more sinister and ominous. Could Wesley have killed Owen out of anger? Fear of being fired? She pulled up the collar of her jacket, coaxed Hoover away from the fire hydrant, and walked quickly down the street. Maybe Selma was still in the shop, doing paperwork and straightening bolts of fabric. Po could pick up a blade for her rotary cutter so that she could cut the rest of the pieces for her star tomorrow. And she'd calm down a bit, too, before she headed home.

It was Susan who answered her light tap at the door and slid the bolt to the side. "Po and Hoover," she said, bending over and scratching the dog behind the ears. "What a nice surprise."

"I thought Selma might still be here and I could pick up a rotary cutter blade."

"No, she's not here, but I'll get you the blade. Eleanor dragged Selma off to the opera in Kansas City. Not exactly Selma's cup of tea but Eleanor insisted she get out of town for a night. I think she's right. And they were going to go to Arthur Bryant's for barbecue before the performance."

"That will do the trick, even if the opera doesn't."

"Yes."

"What are you doing here so late, Susan?"

"I thought I'd catch up on some things for Selma," she said.

"Selma told me you often do that . . . stay late to help her."

"Sometimes," she said quickly. "Not so often really."

"It's nice of you. I'd think you'd have better things to do on a Saturday night." Susan ignored Po's comment. She found the blade on the supplies rack and took it to the counter.

"Shall I charge this?" she asked.

"That would be fine. Now that you mention it, I didn't bring a purse."

"Po," Susan paused and looked at Po. Her eyes were moist. She took a deep breath of air.

"Yes, Susan?" Po noticed that the pen in her hand was shaking slightly.

"Po, I need to talk to you." The words seemed to stick

painfully in her throat.

Po waited, wanting to give her the time she needed. Whatever she wanted to say was difficult, Po could see that.

Suddenly Hoover, who had been lying behind the counter next to Susan, stood at attention, his tail straight and his ears back. His nose lifted into the air.

Susan dropped the pencil and Po looked around. Then they heard it, too. An insistent rattling at the back door, then the sound of door opening and slamming shut.

"Who's there?" Susan called out. Po moved to grab Hoover's leash.

The women heard him before they saw him. The hardwood floor creaked beneath the uneven, slow-moving gait of the large, bulbous body.

"What y'all doing here so late?" Wesley Peet stood in the archway, a crooked grin on his ruddy face.

"Wesley, you're not supposed to come in here," Susan said. Her voice was controlled and even, but her fear was visible in the tight hold of her head and her clenched fists.

"My job's to check on you, pretty lady," he slurred. His eyes were half-shut, his head held back as if to see Susan beneath the partially closed lids. Thin strands of greased hair were slicked back over the pink dome of his head. "Besides, who cares now?"

"As I understand it, your job is to check on the stores from the outside, Wesley," Po said. "Unless there is some disturbance inside. Perhaps you should leave now."

Wesley's eyes stayed on Susan's face. He moved a step closer. "Getting cold out there. You'd better bundle up, Susie-Q." He put his round hands on the counter, his eyes traveling over Susan's body. "You need someone to keep you warm now, don't you, Miss Susan?"

Hoover growled and slunk down next to Po.

Po patted the dog's head and looked hard at Wesley, trying to gauge the level of inebriation. Her eyes took in the dirt beneath his stubby, broken nails and a snake tattoo that curled in and out between his fingers. A dirty white T-shirt peaked out beneath the open front of his blue security uniform, and the stench of sweat, mixed with the sour odor of liquor and stale food, was sickening. "It's good of you to check on us, but we're fine." Po stretched her five-foot-eight frame to capacity.

"I ain't leaving yet," he said. His lips curled.

"Do you want to get fired?" Susan asked, her voice lifting to an uncomfortable level. Hoover bared his teeth.

Sloppy, loud laughter filled the room. Wesley Peet shoved his hands into his pocket and swayed back and forth. "Fired? Now that's a laugh. And who's gonna fire me? Professor Hill? Lawyer Elliott?"

Po could feel his lurid, thick laughter in her bones. She took a step backward and shoved one hand into the pocket of her jeans. Her fingers curled around her cell phone. The movement drew Wesley's stare her way.

"None of you can fire me, Ms. Portia. I know all about you sewing ladies, for sure I do. That's my job. Wesley Peet's protection agency. And Wesley hisself is the most protected of all. Sometimes it pays to be . . ."

He looked around the room as if he'd find the word he wanted lined up next to the bolts of cotton sheeting. Then he focused back on the two women, lifted a finger in the air as if testing the direction of the wind, and spit out his sentence: ". . . sometimes it pays to be curious!" Wesley began to laugh again, harder and harder, and leaned so far to one side that Po was sure he would topple over and become a giant unconscious puddle on the floor. But instead, he righted himself, pulling a hand out of his pocket and grasping a display rack for balance. Feeling secure, he took a step toward Susan and rubbed one grubby finger along her arm.

Susan recoiled, pulling her arm to her chest.

"That's it . . . out of here!" Po grabbed a long pair of scissors from the desk and held it up in the air. "Out!" she yelled. "Now." With that, Hoover leapt into action and rushed toward Wesley Peet, his tail swinging and his white teeth ready for flesh.

Wesley's retreat took seconds. The slam of the back door and crunch of gravel as he ran down the alley assured Po and Susan that he wouldn't be back.

"What an awful man," Po said, sinking into a chair.

"A drunk, awful man." Susan's face was pale.

"There's no question about keeping him on," Po said. "You need to tell Selma tomorrow, and she needs to get him fired. And if you don't, Susan, I will."

Susan nodded, turning off the computer. "Po, I don't want you walking home. I'm leaving now. I'll drive you."

"But I have Hoover . . .," Po began. Hoover's ears picked up. He was sitting next to Po, his head cocked with pride for his recent successful chase.

"Don't be silly. Hoover's welcome to ride in my car, if he can stand the back seat mess. Come on, I can finish this tomorrow." She grabbed a ring of keys and her jacket, turned out the lights and locked the door, and they headed for her car.

"This is nice of you, Susan. I run in this neighborhood all the time, but walking home alone tonight may have been uncomfortable." She settled into the front seat of Susan's red Ford Escort while Hoover happily curled up with a stack of books in the back.

"Sometimes I think my whole life is in this car," Susan said, glancing back at a pair of sneakers, piles of notebooks, papers, books and assorted bags. She patted Hoover's head as he stuck his nose into an old grocery bag.

"You've a busy life," Po said. "I remember when the kids were little, the car held clothes, food, homework, and many things I'd hate to mention." They turned the corner at Windsor House and Po glanced down the alley and spotted Wesley getting into a truck parked beneath the lone alley lamppost. "Looks like Wesley got a new truck." She pointed toward the shiny Dodge Ram.

Susan slowed down and looked. "He was driving a beat-up old Chevy last I noticed. Do you suppose he won the lottery?"

"I hope so. It may make up for the job he's about to lose," Po said. She rested her head back against the seat.

Susan pulled to a stop in Po's driveway and Po slipped out of the car. She opened the back door for Hoover, who immediately ran around to the back yard. Po watched his tail disappear behind the house.

"Well, at least he waited until we got home to do his thing." She leaned a little further into the car. "Susan, thank you. If I can ever do anything for you . . ." Her words hung

Goose Chase

in the air. "If you want to talk?" Susan hadn't picked up on the conversation Wesley had interrupted. And during the drive home, Po could tell that she had moved beyond it and was unlikely to return, at least tonight.

"Thank you, Po," was all she said.

"Well, I'm here." Po watched with an unexplainable heavy heart as Susan drove off into the night, to what seemed to Po to be a burdened, lonely life.

♦

CHAPTER 17

Wild Goose Chase

Sam Paltrow had started the Sunday supper tradition before the ink was dry on their marriage certificate. Po loved being in the kitchen — so Sam decided he'd love it, too. While Po experimented with wine-flavored sauces and seafood pastas, Sam mastered mixing dry martinis and grilling slabs of ribs, trout, and steaks on the grill. Friends, family, neighbors — and sometimes near-strangers who needed a warm meal and spirited conversation — ended up at

"Sam's suppers," as they came to be called. But no one entering the house at 22 Maple Lane ever stayed a stranger for long. Both Sam and Po made sure of that.

After Sam died, Po never for a minute thought about discontinuing the suppers. Oh, she missed a Sunday now and then because she was traveling or a book deadline loomed, but to stop the tradition wouldn't have felt right, plain and simple

Po fussed around in the kitchen late Sunday afternoon, wondering who would show up tonight. She was sure of Kate, who rarely missed and usually managed to sneak out at the end of the evening with enough leftovers for a week's worth of lunches. Tonight Kate arrived with P.J. in tow, which pleased Po greatly, though she'd never admit as much. He wore jeans and a crisp chambray shirt, rolled halfway up his forearms. His flop of thick brown hair was carefully brushed and slightly damp from a recent shower. Po put him to work immediately preparing the coals outside while she placed a huge piece of plump, fresh salmon in a dill wine marinade.

"So tell me, Kate," Po said, washing her hands at the sink, "has P.J. Flanigan mellowed since his wild youth?"

"Like a fine French wine," Kate said. She grabbed a cutting board and a handful of carrots from a strainer in the sink. "I'd say if he mellowed any more, he'd be asleep standing in those size 14 shoes." She wrinkled her nose at Po and began chopping the carrots into tiny pieces.

"Watch your fingers, Kate." Po turned the burner down beneath the lemon butter sauce for the asparagus. "Now what does that face mean?"

"It means that even without my mother beside you, you're

still a meddlin' woman, Po Paltrow."

Po's husky laugh mingled with the faint strains of Vivaldi's "The Four Seasons" coming from the stereo. "And I can see you haven't forgotten how to put me in my place. Now, dear heart, back to P.J. What was that that Phoebe called him awhile back?"

"Man candy," Eleanor called out, coming in from the hallway, her cane tip-tapping on the hardwood floor. "And you really ought to consider locking your front door." She dropped her cane beside a dining chair and sat down.

"And why would I do that, Eleanor? Then people like you might not walk in."

Eleanor was wearing her signature wide-legged pants. Tonight it was paired with a purple silk T-shirt and a silk scarf around her neck. She had added a jaunty hat that sat loosely on her cap of steel gray hair. "Here," she said, placing a bottle of Chardonnay on the table.

"This is my contribution. Not all of us can quilt after drinking your martinis, Po, and I have some work to do on my star when I get home."

"And some of us can't quilt before drinking her martinis," Kate groaned. "I worked on mine this morning and my corners look more like roundabouts!"

"You'll get the hang of it, Kate," Eleanor encouraged. "Take it from one who knows. It has taken me thirty years to get my corners square. I think I want that on my tombstone. "Here lies Eleanor. Her corners were square."' Eleanor's contagious laughter was deep, throaty and filled with more than eight decades of an adventurous life.

"Well, I'm not quilting tonight, so I'll have a martini,"

Po said. "You two pick your poison and make sure P.J. has whatever his handsome heart desires."

By the time the threesome had the vegetables cut, the orzo ready to boil in a peppery broth, and a batch of martinis chilling in the refrigerator, the doorbell was ringing. August Schuette and his wife Rita had arrived. Rita carried a platter of plump mushrooms filled with creamy crab. Leah came, too, along with her husband Tim.

Before long the kitchen area was filled with people, appetizers and animated talk. Phoebe and Jimmy came with the twins, who were immediately scooped up and passed around by eager arms anxious to hug the babies or to sit on the floor and catch them as they groped their way around the furniture.

Kate followed Po out to the patio. A snappy breeze whipped her hair around her high cheekbones. Like P.J., she wore jeans tonight, and a cobalt blue cashmere that Po had given her for Christmas. She wrapped her arms around her soft sweater and snuggled in its warmth.

P.J. stopped and watched the two women walk toward him. He welcomed them with outstretched arms and a smile. "How rich a man am I," he said dramatically.

"The cornball kid," Po said. "Some things don't change no matter how much they mellow or age."

Kate laughed and P.J. looked confused but brushed it off as a ladies' private joke. "Fire's ready, Po. Bring on the salmon. This man's ready to grill."

Po handed him the platter. "It's all yours, P.J." She set the sauce on the table next to the grill. "By the way, P.J., is there any update on the hit and run?"

"Not much," P.J. said. He teased the coals with a metal fork and they jumped to life. "Someone else confirmed that it was twilight, probably the worst time to see details. I checked on Max earlier and the news is still bad."

"While Leah and I were having breakfast at Marla's today, some members of All Saints church came in after the service," Po said. "They said Mary attended, but that she was pale and shaky. What a blow this must have been to her."

"Reverend Gottrey and his wife went with the officer to tell her. They knew it'd be tough, Max being her husband's best friend and all." P.J. said.

"My neighbor is a nurse at the hospital and said Mary calls hourly to see how Max is doing." Kate added. "She's sent enough flowers to fill a church. I don't know if Mary can take losing someone else so close to her."

"P.J., has anyone talked to the security guard that works for the Elderberry shops?" Po felt guilty even saying the words. Accusing — or even suspecting — someone of murder was an outrageous thing to do. But Wesley Peet scared her and there was something not right about him. "It seems Owen was about to fire Wesley before he died," she went on, "and Max was the self-appointed guardian of Owen's unfinished tasks. Wesley is an unsavory fellow, P.J. He scared Susan and me last night, and I don't scare easily."

"Kill two people for a menial job? That's a weak motive, Po."

"I suspect people have killed for less, P.J. Besides, Wesley must have been well paid. Susan and I saw him drive off in a fancy new truck last night."

"What happened to his old truck?"

Po shrugged.

"We've started a list of folks with old trucks who knew Max. You'd be amazed. Everyone from a disgruntled client to Daisy Sample — who wasn't too fond of Max or Owen — to big old Wesley, who may or may not still have his old truck. Even Maggie has an old truck. There's a cast of thousands."

"Trucks are big here."

"I don't have a truck," Kate said.

P.J. looped an arm across her shoulder. "Good to hear that, Katie. I guess I can cross you off my suspect list."

"Don't be too hasty, P.J. Everyone is a suspect." She dipped her finger in the remains of the basting sauce. "Po — that's a great sauce."

Po smiled absently. She was still thinking about the trucks, and the connections between the two men, Owen and Wesley, and something that niggled at her mind like a fly in the bedroom at night, but she couldn't quite figure what it was.

Sam's suppers brought out the best in folks, and conversations often ran rampant. But the most heated talk tonight was about Wesley Peet and the scare he had given Susan and Po. "Something has to be done about that man," Rita Schuette said. Born in Columbia, Rita had beautiful olive skin, a flawless, youthful complexion, and a fiery disposition that some found daunting, but Po thought enchanting. Tonight her black eyes blazed.

Gus agreed. "Ambrose seems to think he's doing okay. And he's cheap."

Cheap? Po thought. Well, cheap didn't buy a brand new truck, but she held the thought to herself for now, not wanting to spread such talk until she had had time to think about it.

"Po, where's Kate?" P.J. asked. He was carrying a plate heaped high with apple pie and the homemade ice cream Po had made that afternoon.

Po looked around. "I saw her awhile ago, talking to Phoebe on the patio. I think they were planning a lynching of Wesley Peet for scaring us."

Jimmy came up beside P.J., balancing Jude on one hip and cradling a sleeping Emma on his shoulder. "I can't find Phoebe, either."

Po frowned. She didn't trust those two. Especially not with Phoebe's newfound zest for Mission Impossible schemes. At least she wasn't wearing her cat outfit tonight. "Maybe they went down to pick up something at the store," she said aloud.

"Maybe," Jimmy said. "But I can't imagine what."

It was thirty minutes later, after Eleanor and most of the others had gone on home, when Phoebe and Kate wandered in. Their cheeks were flushed and Kate had that look in her eyes that Po remembered from years ago when she'd skipped class. Or sneaked out at night with a friend and climbed a roof to watch the stars. Her mother would call Po, worried sick, while Kate's dad scoured the neighborhood. Hours later, Kate would wander in, innocent and yawning, and wondering what all the fuss was about.

"Kate?" Po said. The single word demanded a response.

Kate kissed her on the cheek. "Sorry, Po. Phoebe and I had something we had to take care of."

"Kate Simpson, where were you?" Po eyes never left Kate's flushed face.

Phoebe looked up. She had curled up in one of Po's overstuffed chairs in front of the fire. Jude was on her lap, happily nursing his missed dinner. "Oh, Po, don't fuss. We ran down to Elderberry Road to see a man about a horse."

"A man about a truck," Kate corrected. "What we did was satisfy our curiosity. We went down to check out Wesley's truck, to see if we could find anything inside that might let us know what he was up to. The way he acted with you and Susan was horrible. We thought maybe we'd find something incriminating."

"And what exactly would that be? That's downright foolish, Kate," P.J. said. "Wesley Peet could be dangerous. What's more, it's illegal. You don't go breaking into people's private property."

Jimmy was glaring at Phoebe from across the room. Jude sucked away happily.

"We didn't break in. It sounds more foolish that it was," Kate said quietly. "Marla told us that Wesley always takes a break at nine. He walks over to that Seven Eleven on Pine Street and has a smoke because Mary Hill won't let him smoke in the alley. So we checked his truck out while he was gone. It was locked but the back window wasn't latched . . ."

"So Phoebe crawled through," Jimmy muttered.

"Kate stayed at the end of the alley and watched in case he came back. It wasn't dangerous. Just futile. There wasn't much there."

Po sat down opposite Phoebe in a matching chair. This room always wrapped people in a warm, cozy feeling. Tonight it was as chilly as the first snow.

CHAPTER 18

Sawtooth Edge

Before she went to bed, Po drank a cup of tea that Rita Schuette had brought to her that day. It was a special blend, Rita said, guaranteed to make you sleep. And whatever magic had been in the tea leaves, it worked. Somewhere, far off, she had heard sirens during the early morning hours. But they were hazy and far away — more dreamlike than real — and Po never rose above the sweet blanket of sleep. She woke up Monday morning more refreshed than she had been since all the Elderberry Road trouble began.

Today she had a mission to carry out, and thanks to Rita's tea, she was feeling up to it. After two cups of coffee and a productive hour at the computer working on her book, Po set out for Elderberry Road.

The day was crisp and cold. Football weather, Gus had called it the night before. Po had pulled on a deep purple Guatemalan jacket that a friend had given her. She snuggled her cheek against the thick collar, welcoming its woolly warmth. Winter was a hair's breadth away. Po walked quickly, breathing in the morning air, and mentally reviewing her case for the firing of Wesley Peet.

Po wondered if Wesley was a police suspect. He had a motive for the killings, however weak P.J. might consider it. He was about to lose his job. And who else would hire such a burly, unsavory fellow? Po quickened her pace — she wanted to reach the shops before they opened for business. As she neared Mary Hill's store, Po decided that she would approach Ambrose first. She'd pull him aside to tell him about her frightening encounter with Wesley Peet. And then they'd talk about what could be done.

As she turned the corner onto Elderberry Road, Po stopped short and tried to make sense of the scene ahead. A small group of curious people were gathered on the curb in front of Windsor House Antiques: a mother with two small children, a scattering of students, several well-dressed people on their way to offices nearby.

They were all staring at Mary Hill's plate glass display window. At first Po thought maybe she had created a new display, perhaps brought the extraordinary collection of paperweights in front where passers-by could enjoy their beauty. But as Po got closer, she spotted the reason for the crowd's curiosity. It wasn't a dazzling display of art, but instead, a jagged hole, the size of a baseball, that marred the huge expanse of glass. Spiraling out in all directions were tiny star-like lines, etched in the broken glass and glistening in the morning sun. On the other side of the window, work-men moved lamps and chairs and picture frames away from the window. Po spotted Gus Schuette walking toward her from his store down the street.

"Gus, what happened here?"

Gus's face was pinched, his brows pulled together tightly, "Someone threw a glass ball through Mary's window. Damn crazy fool. It sure isn't what that lady needs in her life right now."

"It's not what any of you need. This is awful, Gus. Where's Mary?"

"She's inside. In denial, I think. She probably wouldn't have even called the police if the alarm hadn't gone off when the window was hit. The cops have come and gone. Said it was a drive-by prank, most likely. Kids out too late with nothing better to do." Gus took Po by the elbow and led her around a gawking bystander, down the alley, and in the back-door of the antique shop.

"Mary?" Gus called out. "Where are you? It's Gus and Po." Mary emerged from a small office in the back of the store. She was dressed impeccably, as always, but her oval face was as white as the lace pillows on the antique bed beside the door. Her smile was forced. "Isn't this a mess?" she asked with feigned brightness. Her hands spread out to take in the moved furniture, the tiny sparkles of glass on the floor. "Now why would anyone think this was fun?"

"It's not fun, it's terrible, Mary. Do you think it was a prank?" Po asked. With the ominous cloud that hovered over Elderberry Road, Po's thoughts were far more sinister.

Mary's shoulders shrugged in her silk taupe blouse. "What else?" She watched two workmen carefully remove the panel of glass. Cold air blew into the store and Mary shivered involuntarily. "The workmen will replace it immediately. Fortunately Owen put in the best protective glass money can buy. That's why it's only the single hole and not an entire smashed window. There's really little mess." Mary chattered on about the window and the film that protected it. The fact that someone had assaulted her store didn't seem to have sunk in yet. Po hoped Mary would be all right when it did.

"What did you say was thrown?" Po asked. She looked at Gus. "The hole looks like it might have been a rock or a baseball."

"Yes," Mary said. "It doesn't matter. What's done is done. I thank you both for coming by, but it will be fine. I would prefer we just get it cleaned up and move on." She forced a smile. "Business as usual."

Po and Gus took their cue and left the store. They walked down the alley toward the bookstore. "Gus, this isn't right," she said. "I don't think Mary gets it. Do you think it was just a prank?"

"I think we need a cup of coffee." He steered Po into the back door of Marla's shop, through the tiny kitchen, heated with the enticing aroma of freshly baked bread, and into the dining area. "Marla, two coffees," he called out as they settled down at a round table near the window. The shop was busy but not full, and Marla spotted them immediately. She swung her large body around the bakery case and made her way slowly to their table.

"What's next?" she asked, filling their cups. "Plagues? Locusts?"

"It's awful, Marla. What have you heard?"

"I've heard that we all need bullet-proof glass. What's this world coming to?" Her round cheeks were bright red and drops of perspiration beaded her wide brow. "Scares me, Gus," she said, looking at the bookstore owner. "We need to do something."

"It seems you could improve on security, for one thing," Po said. "Where was Wesley Peet when all this happened?"

"He's only here until one. The police said the alarm went off about one-thirty or two. But no matter, Mary Hill sure gave Wesley a piece of her mind this morning. She was chewing him out in the alley something fierce when I came in to turn on the ovens." Marla set the pot down on the table and pulled out a chair, maneuvering her large body onto the cushion. "I didn't think she had it in her, always so refined and quiet, that one. But she was as wound up as a Kansas tornado this morning." She looked at Gus again. "Maybe we should have Wesley stay around all night?"

"Maybe you should have someone who doesn't drink his way through his shift," Po suggested.

"I heard about that little episode Saturday night," Marla said. "You're right, Po. He needs to stay off the booze. Don't think he would hurt anyone, though, but maybe we should think about it," she conceded. "Something sure has to be done to calm things down around here. I'm so jumpy I dropped a whole platter of cinnamon rolls on the floor this morning." She pulled herself up from the table, took back her coffee pot, and walked off toward the kitchen, shaking her head and mumbling to herself.

"Did you say it was a glass ball that caused the damage?"

"That's what one of the cops said. Looked like a paper-weight, he said."

Po frowned. How odd. She thought of the extraordinary Perthshire glass balls that graced the display cabinet. But the ball came from the other side. Curious.

Gus drained his coffee cup and put it back on the table. He shoved back his chair. "I'm off, Po. I have a new salesperson starting today and need to get myself organized."

"Business must be good?"

"Pretty good. This nasty mess surrounding Owen still hovers over all of us. But otherwise it's good. I don't happen to agree with the police that the college kids are out pulling pranks, like smashing Mary's window. Those kids are good to me. Studious, for the most part, and they sure buy a lot of books."

Po agreed. "There's always a bad apple or two, but that's true in any group. Even in this neighborhood."

"Yeah, for sure. Bad apples everywhere." Gus waved and left the way he came, through the kitchen and out the back door. Po sat at the table for a while, barely noticing when the waitress refilled her mug and Marla plunked a thick slice of French toast in front of her. Her head was filled to overflow-ing with broken windows, lifeless bodies, and hit and runs. She thought about this latest twist of events, and about all the loose strings that were fluttering around as irritating as gnats. She wondered if they would ever come together.

This latest threat — if that's what it was — was one more wayward puzzle piece. Surely no one was out to get both the Hills. It didn't make sense. But neither did Mary's odd reaction to the window damage. She seemed eerily calm, not the Mary that Marla described, berating the security guard for his lapse of attention. Did Mary think her life was in danger? You wouldn't have guessed that easily.

Po sipped her coffee slowly and picked at the French toast. Somehow she didn't have much of an appetite anymore. She was convinced there was a connection between Owen and Max's misfortunes. And an uncomfortable, niggling feeling told her that the shattering of Mary's window should not be discounted quite so quickly.

Po glanced out the window and for a short moment, her breath caught tight in her chest.

Wesley Peet sat on the wooden bench just outside Marla's café. His huge, muscular body filled the seat and a look of fierce concentration filled his face. Enormous boots were planted firmly on the sidewalk, his elbows leaning so hard on his knees that Po thought they would surely cause dents. A small, crooked smile lifted the edges of his fat lips. His head was turned slightly, and from where Po sat, it looked like his beady, black eyes were staring down Windsor House Antiques.

Po shivered. Then, as she watched, Wesley rose from the bench and lumbered across the street toward his shiny new truck.

The truck Phoebe and Kate had foolishly entered the night before. Po sat still, staring after him, long after the truck had disappeared around the corner and out of sight.

"A penny for your thoughts."

Po looked up into Kate Simpson's smile.

Po smiled back. "Kate, you're a welcome sight. Can you sit?"

Kate pulled out a chair and sat down. She turned over her cup. "I'm playing hooky today. I told them I couldn't sub, and instead I plan to curl up in one of Gus's chairs with my trusty laptop and finish my midterm paper."

"Gus was just here, as a matter of fact." Po pushed her uneaten toast in Kate's direction. "He and I have had an interesting morning."

The waitress walked over, filled both mugs with coffee and disappeared.

"Don't keep me in suspense," Kate said.

Kate listened intently, devouring the French Toast, but leaving her large brown eyes fastened on Po's face, as Po related her version of the morning's events, from the smashing of the window to watching Wesley on the park bench. When she was finished, Kate sat back in the chair and wiped drops of syrup from the corner of her mouth. Her eyes were wide.

"Well? What do you make of it all?" Po asked.

Kate's voice was edged with excitement. "Po, this is downright creepy. Remember Phoebe and my little sleuthing episode last night?"

"Your illegal breaking and entering, you mean?"

"Whatever. Well, we told you we didn't find anything. And we didn't think we did — but we did see something we both thought a bit odd."

"Well?"

"Well . . ." Kate dragged out the single word, then continued. "On the back seat of his truck was a small box. Phoebe didn't see it when she crawled through the window and she knocked it onto the floor. The lid fell off, and this thing rolled out."

Po didn't like pursuing this because she thought Kate had done a terribly foolish thing breaking into that truck. Listening to her talk about it somehow spoke of approval. But curiosity — and the light in Kate's eyes — got the best of her. "And what was the thing, Kate?"

"It was a beautiful glass ball, about the size of a baseball."

CHAPTER 19

Drunkard's Path

Wesley Peet shuffled down the dark alley, a flashlight in one hand and an amber pint bottle in the other. The beam of his flashlight traveled unevenly in and out of the narrow dark spaces between buildings. He paused near a dumpster and leaned against the metal side, his head pleasantly woozy.

Couldn't take these late nights much longer, he thought, wiping the dripping liquor from his wet mouth with the back of his hand. Hell, he wouldn't have to take these late nights much longer. Life was lookin' good for old Wesley for the first time in forty years. He lifted the pint of Chivas Regal to his lips and took a long swig, then stared at the bottle in the dim light. The Scotch itself was an omen that everything was finally turning around for old Wesley Peet. There it stood by its lonesome, just outside the pitch-black wine store, sitting on the step saying, "Wesley, take me. I'm yours." His laughter gurgled up from deep in the back of his throat, and when it stopped, he took another long, slow draw from the bottle, savoring the taste.

Ambrose Sweet must have left the bottle there by accident, probably meant to take it home to that fancy house of his, but hell, he sure wouldn't miss it, not with a store crammed with the stuff. Wesley had helped himself to a small bottle or two in the past, slipping it into his pants pocket when he checked out the storage room. But he'd never have touched this pricey stuff, yet there it was, just waiting for him. It sure beat the rotten swill he usually drank. And from the bottle alone, he knew this hooch had to cost a buck or two. Wesley smiled crookedly. Yeah, it was a good sign for Wesley Peet. Bright, sunshiny days ahead. And bucks to burn.

He'd been smart for once in his useless life — done what was good for Wesley and the hell with the rest. What had the world ever done for him anyhow? He'd taken care of every-thing this time, showed 'em who was boss. Couldn't pull the wool over old Wesley, not on your life. He sure proved that.

Wesley stumbled down the empty alley, his head so full of thoughts that he didn't see the old truck parked at the end of the alley, just across the street from the antique place. But if he had seen it, he wouldn't have given it much thought. Just another truck parked at the curb, somebody visiting somebody, somebody spending the night.

He checked the round watch on his wrist and focused hard until the numbers stopped jumping around. Midnight. He'd just leave a little early tonight, take the rest of that bottle back to his place and have his own little celebration. Who cares? Who'd rob this place? This was a place to get murdered, not robbed. He giggled foolishly at his own attempt at humor and snapped on his flashlight, pointing it at the back door of the quilt shop.

Right there, he thought. His flashlight formed a perfect circle of light on the step, like a spotlight on a stage, waiting for someone to step into it. Or to fall dead in it.

Maybe Owen Hill didn't know it, Wesley thought, but there were worse things in life than getting wasted in a quilt shop. He could tell him a tale or two about growing up with a boozin' father and no mother to speak of. Brawls, beatings. Owen Hill sure didn't know about that. Bump on the head, go to sleep. Besides, he'd sure had his little pleasures, hadn't he? A life full of 'em, Wesley suspected. And now it was Wesley's turn. The new truck was already his, but that was just the beginning. Now that he'd proved he meant business — that no one could fool old Wesley Peet . . . hah! — now the real payoff would come. Tomorrow. All arranged. All set. And Wesley'd be off into the sunset, a happy man at last. Mexico maybe? No Kansas winters there.

He'd promised to do this one last shift. Then off he'd be. Forever.

The moon was as big as a pumpkin and a crisp breeze tugged off the few remaining leaves on the elm trees. The round beam from Wesley's flashlight wobbled up the back of the brick building that housed the wine shop, up to the slanted roof, then back down again. Wesley took another long drink of Scotch, then lumbered on, nearly stumbling smack into the dumpster behind Daisy Sample's flower shop. The heavy metal lid was open, held up by the metal brace. Wesley stared up at it, curious why the flower lady'd done that, left it open like that. He hadn't noticed it on his way down the alley earlier. Fighting hard against the fuzz in his head, he shined his flashlight up to the lid, then down, and looked into the deep belly of the trash bin. Almost empty, he thought. His flashlight traveled over a couple of cardboard boxes and packing foam. Then stopped short. There at the bottom, scattered around on top of one of the boxes, were several bills.

He peered closer. "Hundred smackers!" he said aloud. Damn! It *is* his lucky night. He looked around, spotted one of Daisy's flower crates, and pulled it to the edge of the bin, then hoisted his huge body up onto it and leaned over the edge of the dumpster. His head was filled with cotton but not enough to blot out the thrill of found money. He chuckled softly as his fat fingers fumbled for the bills. He didn't need the money now, but old habits die hard, as his old man used to say. There, two fingers touched the first one hundred dollar bill and curled around it.

At first, the crunching gravel went unnoticed, blotted out by the excitement of the treasure he'd found. Wesley leaned a little further into the bin and reached for another bill.

He wrapped his fingers around it and only then did he hear the sound, distinct now, closer. This time it was right next to him. He pulled his head up and looked to the side.

Their eyes met, and Wesley knew right then and there that

there would be no Mexico. Nada. He'd been duped. His old man had been right all along. Stupid kid. Worthless, shiftless excuse for a human being. Would never amount to anything. In the distance Wesley heard another noise, one he recognized — the incessant barking of that foolish mutt across the fence.

And then everything turned black as the heavy metal lid of the dumpster came crashing down on Wesley Peet's head.

◆

CHAPTER 20

Barn Raising

Wesley Peet's murder was too late to make the Tuesday morning paper, but the local television station reported it hourly as "breaking news." By noon, the town was alive with speculation. Po heard it through her Walkman earphones as she ran along the river. As the first burst of news traveled through the thin wires, she stopped dead in her tracks and moaned. She leaned forward from the waist, her hands on her hips. Perspiration dripped from her forehead.

"Oh, my," Po murmured as her heart sank down into her running shoes. The investigative reporter on the radio continued her detailed account, telling Po that at first, police thought Wesley's death was a tragic accident — a uniformed security guard examining suspect refuse in a dumpster, was hit on the head by the heavy lid when a broken support latch collapsed. It crushed the man's skull, causing immediate death.

But after careful examination, the reporter announced, clearly pleased her story didn't end on such a note, the police determined that it was not an accident: The man's blood's alcohol level was a whopping .13, he was scavenging for money in the metal garbage bin, and his death appeared to be a planned execution.

Po pulled the earphones out and looped them around her neck. Execution. Good grief. What was this, The Untouchables? She held one tiny earphone back to her ear and learned that a bottle of pricey Scotch whiskey was found nearby. A bit out of his league, Po thought.

Po also learned that Wesley had a ticket confirmation in his pocket for a flight to Mexico two days off, that he was trying to lay claim to several one-hundred dollar bills lying on the bottom of the dumpster when he met his untimely demise, and that he had worked for the Elderberry Shop corporation for several months.

This time Po groaned out loud.

"Po, is that you?"

Po looked up. A small silver Passat idled at the curb near the end of the running path.

Leah leaned through the open window. "I can see by the look on your face that you've heard the news."

Po wiped the perspiration from her brow with the small towel around her neck. She wasn't sure which had caused her heart to race so — the running or the news. "How much more can those poor folks take, Leah?"

"I don't know. Selma must be beside herself. I was going to go over there tonight anyway. Care to join me?"

Po assured her that she did. And knowing Kate would want to be there, too, she called her after showering and dressing, and left a message on her answering machine.

They all showed up, of course, just as Po knew they would. Kate had called Phoebe and Maggie. Leah had stopped by Eleanor's.

"So, you ladies need some extra quilting time?" Selma asked, and then she allowed herself to fall into Po's tight embrace.

"Here," Maggie said. "I've brought food." She set a large, colorful platter in the middle of the table. The ceramic plate was glazed to a high sheen, but the real point of interest was its shape — a large, beautiful woman, lying on her back and floating serenely in some invisible sea. She wore a bright red bikini and sunglasses, and her wide, round arms, her shapely hands and painted nails formed a rim around the edge of the platter. In the center, an ample pink belly held a platter full of Maggie's homemade chocolate chip cookies. Two giant breasts, covered in a bikini top, watched guard over the cookies.

Phoebe collapsed in laughter. The others paraded around

the table, viewing the newest piece of Maggie's art with great delight.

"And her name?" Kate asked between giggles.

"Madame Cookie, of course," Maggie answered, "My sister found her at the Plaza Art Fair in Kansas City last month. Couldn't resist her."

"Of course she couldn't," Selma said. "Who could?"

"She's worthy of carrying your chocolate chip cookies, Maggie, and I wouldn't say that about just anyone." Leah grabbed a warm cookie off the plate.

Maggie blew her a kiss.

"Well, I brought something, too," said Phoebe. She walked over to the back door, opened it, and pulled inside an easel with a giant pad of white paper on it. "Jimmy bought this for the twins, but since it'll be a couple years before they can use it, he loaned it to us."

"For a Queen Bees' crime briefing," Po said. "Phoebe, you're a genius."

"I figure we've all been sleuthing like crazy and it's time to put thoughts to paper." She stretched out the easel legs until the board was steady and pulled out a pack of marking pens. "Okay, so let's start with you, Kate. What does P.J. say about this latest development?"

In minutes the Queen Bees had gathered around the table, munching on cookies and sipping the coffee Selma had put on when she saw them coming. Phoebe stood at the end, scribbling comments on the large white sheet of paper.

The police didn't know what to think, Kate admitted. P.J. had tracked her down and called her out of class that day, wanting to make sure she was okay. And then he'd filled her in. There were no fingerprints on anything, he said, so who ever had released the lid of the dumpster knew exactly what he was doing. The only other thing they found was the bottle of Scotch. And it was covered with fingerprints. All Wesley's.

"That's odd," Po said. "Someone had to give him the bottle."

"P.J. said a kid from the Elderberry neighborhood saw the bottle when he rode his bike through the alley on his way home around eight o'clock. It was sitting outside the wine store on the steps."

"Odd place for a pint of Scotch. Someone must have put it there and wiped it clean," Po said.

"Someone like Ambrose or Jesse? They're the only ones who sell good Scotch around here." Selma walked around the table with her coffeepot. She was more at ease when moving, less anxious when there were tasks to be done.

"And it was their store," Maggie added.

"But why would they leave it outside? Everyone knows Wesley is a rumpot." Phoebe scratched her head.

"Someone may have wanted him to have it. To get tipsy." Maggie frowned, then decided she may have hit on something. "If he was tipsy, he couldn't fight back. Wesley was a frightful brute and could have beaten anyone off. I think it would have been a wise move to get him drunk, lure him to the dumpster, then smash! It's all over."

Kate frowned. "But why would anyone want Wesley dead? That's the real issue here. He was an unfortunate lush who wasn't very good at his terrible job, but that really doesn't merit a terrible death like that. There must have been something else."

Po thought back to the night he frightened her and Susan in the shop. "He said some odd things that night he came into the shop," she said aloud. "I thought he was speaking nonsense through the haze of the liquor, but he talked about knowing things, being curious. And how it all paid off. The way he talked about Owen being dead and Max nearly so, made me think he did it. He was about to be fired, he hated Owen Hill — it all fit."

The others nodded.

"But he also talked about being safe, protected," Po continued. "Which means he probably did know something."

"So he was blackmailing someone," Phoebe said, writing BLACKMAIL in huge letters on the white sheet of paper. "Okay, so who?"

"The person who killed Owen and put Max into a coma," Leah said, and Phoebe duly recorded it.

"Daisy was ready to kill Owen," Selma offered. "And Max was picking up the torch."

Phoebe wrote DAISY on the sheet.

Selma looked up at the list. "You might as well put me up there, too, Phoebe. I didn't do it, but I had motive."

"No," Phoebe said simply.

"What about Ambrose and Jesse?" Maggie asked. "They could have put that bottle out to get Wesley snockered, then unlocked the latch as he was hanging over the side trying to get the money. And they both knew Owen was at the shop late that night. They'd have much more control now that he's not the corporation director."

"That's true," Selma admitted. "Owen squelched many of their uppity ideas."

Phoebe added AMBROSE and JESSE to the list.

"I may be struck dead," Eleanor said, "but I think we've forgotten someone important on this list."

"Who's that, Eleanor," Kate asked.

"The Reverend Gottrey. I don't mean to speak ill of a man of the cloth. I happen to think our priest at St. Pats is amazing, wonderful and talks spirituality better than Gandhi and Mother Theresa. But I think the Reverend may have mighty powerful money motives."

"The Owen Hills Spiritual Retreat, the church roof —and those may just be the tip of the treasure," Leah said. "I know he would never be getting that wonderful farm if Owen were alive."

Phoebe drew a steeple on the white sheet of paper. "I just don't feel right printing his name out," she explained.

"I'm fond of Gus," Po said. "But I guess if we're doing this, we should do it right. He belongs up there with the rest of them. Max told me that Owen was calling for an audit of Gus's books. He wanted to be sure he was contributing his fair share to the maintenance fund."

GUS was added to the list.

"Who have we forgotten?" Kate asked.

"Well, if we're adding the whole block," Phoebe said, "I suppose we have to add Mary Hill as well."

They were all silent. Happily married wives killing their terrific husbands was difficult for all of them to swallow. Dutifully, Phoebe wrote MARY on the chart.

"She inherited a bunch of money," Maggie said.

"And I saw her chew out Wesley in the alley yesterday," Selma said. "She was clearly upset with him."

"Wesley may have stole something from her store," Po said. "That may have been why she was angry."

"What would Wesley want from an antique store?" Leah asked.

"One of those beautiful glass paper weights that Mary has on display."

"Isn't that what was thrown through Mary's window?" Eleanor asked.

Po nodded but didn't elaborate about how she knew Wesley stole the glass paperweight. She didn't want to embarrass Phoebe and Kate by telling everyone about their adolescent adventure.

"Phoebe and I found a glass ball in Wesley's truck Sunday night, the night before Mary's shop was vandalized," Kate announced, unabashed. "And I forgot to tell you, Po, but P.J. said they checked it out and, though Wesley may have stolen it from Mary's, it wasn't one of the expensive ones. It was the kind you buy at a fine gift store for forty or fifty dollars. But it was still quite beautiful, P.J. said, and looked a lot like those in Mary's shop."

Po's mind was still on Mary. No one knew what went on between a husband and wife, but Po knew Mary cared deeply about Max. Just this afternoon she had met her coming out of his office. Mary explained she was taking some pictures up to the hospital, things that he might recognize, that might help reconnect him to the world if he comes out of the coma. All this while still dealing with her own pain.

Po frowned, trying desperately to put the puzzle pieces in place. Why would Wesley steal from Mary's store? And more puzzling, why would he vandalize it later? She rested her head on her hands, her elbows on the tabletop and listened with half an ear to the gathering of suspicions and motive. It seemed the more information they pulled together, the less sense any of it made. But something was clearly missing. And they needed to discover it quickly before someone else was killed on Elderberry Road.

"Where's Susan?" Kate said suddenly

"She wasn't feeling very good. I sent her home," Selma explained. "She hasn't been eating much, and I think she's run down. She needs a good night's sleep."

"Run down," Phoebe repeated. "That brings us back to the truck piece of this puzzle. Daisy has a truck. But the others? I can't quite imagine Mary Hill behind the wheel of an old beat-up pick-up."

"Or the Reverend," Eleanor said, reluctantly. "But it isn't that hard to get your hands on a truck if that's your goal."

Kate raised her hand. "Phoebe, it might be time to call it a night. I'm brain-dead."

Phoebe looked at her watch in mock frustration. "Oh, I suppose."

But they had made great strides, they all agreed. And a night to sleep on it might be a good thing.

"Let's all do a little snooping on our own," Eleanor suggested.

"Good idea, El," Phoebe said, collapsing her easel and leaning it against the back wall. "I'll leave this right here. We can e-mail anything that comes up, but by Saturday we should have this solved. Right, Bees?"

They raised their hands in unison. "Right!" And so resolved, the Queen Bees departed for their own hives, pretending for the sake of one another that safety and peace were just around the corner.

CHAPTER 21

Crossroads

When Po got home a short while later, she sat at her
kitchen table and listened to a litany of phone messages —
one from her daughter, telling Po that she and her husband
and baby Jane were coming for Thanksgiving. She smiled.
A joyful note in the middle of all this turmoil. Another message was from Peter, the thirteen-year-old boy who lived
down the street. He didn't have school tomorrow so he'd be
over to mow the lawn, he told her, "like for probably the last
time before winter." Po smiled at the deep man-tone that had
crept into little Peter's voice when she wasn't looking. The

last one was a message from her editor saying the first few chapters were fine. An unexpected pang of disappointment passed through her. She stared at the answering machine, wondering what she had expected to hear. Had she thought there might be a voice-mail message announcing, "Your murderer is Colonel Mustard. He did it in the parlor with a candlestick?" Or P.J. calling with the news that they caught the guy at last — a stranger passing through town. Everyone was safe now.

Po looked at the clock on the kitchen wall. Just eight o'clock. Still early. She glanced at the box of Sleepy Time Tea that Rita Schuette had given her. She had a feeling that sleep would drag its feet tonight and an extra strong cup of Rita's tea might be a good thing.

Hoover was curled up in the corner of the kitchen on his flannel bed, content, safe. Po walked to the den, then back into the kitchen again. She wanted to grasp something tightly in her hands. And she felt so close to doing it. But when she reached for it, it slipped away.

She opened the refrigerator and a thin yellow light fell out across the floor.

Dinner. She hadn't eaten any. Maybe that was the cause of this restless itch. This nagging in the pit of her stomach.

Behind the milk and orange juice on the top shelf of the refrigerator, Po found a large container of home-made chicken soup that she had taken out to thaw a day or so ago, then completely forgotten about. She felt the sides of the Tupperware container. Almost thawed. Perfect. Chicken soup, the perfect antidote for this uncomfortable gnawing inside her. "Chicken Soup for the Restless Soul."

She looked at the size of the container and frowned, wondering what she was thinking about when she'd stored it in a container holding enough for the whole neighborhood. This was soup to be shared. And she'd like some company tonight, she realized suddenly.

Po carried the soup to the sink and began to remove the lid, and then the perfect solution came to her. Susan! She hadn't been eating, and Po's chicken soup had never failed to coax the ill to eat. She'd pack up the soup and several packages of Rita's tea, and maybe a pan of moist cornbread that she had picked up earlier in the day at Marla's. She owed Susan a favor, and this might be just the thing to hurry her on her way to health.

In minutes, Po had packed everything in a large wicker basket, adding a batch of brownies she had frozen for just such an occasion, and she was ready to go. The address Selma gave her was not far at all, just on the other side of the river. Ten minutes on quiet streets.

Po pulled up to the small frame house in the modest neighborhood and smiled. It was exactly what she'd expect Susan's house to look like. Though the yards and houses on the block were small — mostly one-story bungalows — Susan's had that special artistic touch, a rose amidst wild flowers. Deep green shutters set off the small, white house. A shiny brass lamplight at the door was on, spilling light over a small front porch. An old Chinese Maple tree filled the front yard, and the small, neat sidewalk was bordered with low, groomed bushes. When she walked up the porch steps, Po noticed the porch swing and rocker, piled with quilted pillows.

She knocked on the door softly.

Susan answered the door in her robe. Her usually neat hair was slightly mussed. "Po," she said, surprised.

"I'm sorry I didn't call first, Susan, but Selma mentioned you were sick, and I had a sudden need to get out of my house. So here I am. I may not be Jewish, but I make a mean chicken soup." Po lifted the basket.

"How sweet of you." Susan hesitated for a moment, then held the door open so Po could pass. "Forgive my manners. Please come in, Po."

Po stepped into a small, comfortable living room. "I don't want to intrude," she said. But in truth, she wanted just that. She liked Susan Miller, but she knew so little about her, and she suspected that deep down, there was a hidden cache of riches there that she hadn't begun to tap. Maybe no one had.

"My mother's asleep in the back, but it's all right. Nothing wakes her."

Po looked around the neat, comfortable room, but almost immediately her eyes were drawn to a brilliant splash of color on the far wall. "Oh, my," Po said aloud.

She set the basket of food on the counter separating the living room and kitchen, and walked over to the hanging. It was a quilt made of cotton, silk and brocade fabrics. They were cut and stitched in hundreds of irregular shapes and pieced together to form an image of woods and fields. A house or cabin in the center was heavy with thousands of seed beads in the same array of brilliant colors. The collage was beautiful and arresting, lifelike and abstract, all at the same time. Po couldn't take her eyes off it. "Susan, this is amazing. It's so . . . happy."

Susan stood back in the entry to the kitchen. She ran her fingers through her hair, coaxing order to it. Her cheeks flushed at Po's words. "Yes," Susan said softly. "It is happy."

Po squinted her eyes, moved close to the hanging, then stood a few steps back, unable to turn her attention away from the art on the wall. She saw comfort and harmony in it, but there was also something reckless — a reckless joy, she decided, that was it.

"I see where the beads idea for Selma's anniversary quilt came from," Po said. She turned toward Susan. "I am in awe. This should be in a gallery."

"This one is just for me. But I've others." Her face brightened. "In fact, I'm making a small one right now for Maggie. It's for her fat lady collection. It's a sweet round lady holding a black lab. I thought she could put it in the clinic." She ushered Po into a small bedroom off the living room and lifted the square from a table near the bed. It was the size of a small tabletop and had a whole different feeling from the one in the living room, but it was equally wonderful, Po thought, and she knew Maggie would love it.

Susan had used all cotton fabric for Maggie's piece, but in different thicknesses and textures, some smooth and almost silky, some pebbled and grainy. The abstract lady was sitting on a park bench, her wide bosom and ample lap filled with a blue-black pup whose bright red tongue licked at her face. "I took some pictures for this one, then finally found just the right one and made a drawing from it. Then I cut different fabrics to fill in the woman's features and the background. Do you think she'll like it?"

"No. She'll be crazy about it. What talent you have, Susan

Miller, and it's hidden under a bushel basket. But I think that's about to end."

"I think we need some tea," she said, brushing off Po's attention.

"I think that's a grand idea." Po followed her into the other room, settling down on a tall stool at the counter. Susan busied herself at the stove, turning up the flame beneath the teakettle.

"How did you do the large quilt hanging?"

Susan sat opposite the counter and looked at the quilt. "I took a lot of pictures for that one, too. I used them as guides, to plan and structure the piece," she said. "Then I let my heart do the rest, I guess."

Po nodded. She had had her own share of projects of the heart — her books, special quilts she made for her children. They talked for awhile about art and quilts, and Po watched the color creep back into Susan's cheeks. "I think you're on the mend," she said.

Susan nodded. "I'm sure I am. Your visit has been wonderful medicine."

Po wanted to ask Susan a dozen questions — about their unfinished conversation in the shop, about the veil that she could feel dropping over Susan right now, the one that told Po they'd talked enough. Don't get any closer, it said.

"Susan, it's that time," Po stood. "I'm going to leave you to a bowl of soup and a good night's sleep. And I think I'll help myself to the same."

Susan nodded. She was fading a little, she admitted, and she followed Po to the small entryway. Po was about to open the door when a collection of photographs on the wall just inside the door caught her eye. She stopped and looked closer at the simply framed black and white photos. "Are these yours, Susan?"

Susan looked over at the wall and nodded. "Another passion of mine. Now you know everything there is to know about me, Po."

Po didn't answer. She moved closer and looked at each one, wanting to know the Susan of the photographs. These were not snapshots, but wonderfully composed photographs. There was a long, winding country road. A rural crossroads with a field of cows looking curiously at the road signs. A still pond filled with lily pads and surrounded by waving grasses and cattails. The center photo was larger than the others, and Po saw immediately that it was the inspiration for the quilt. The photo was taken at sundown, Po suspected, and amazingly captured the myriad of colors in the falling night sky, but through shades of grays and blacks and whites. It was a country scene like the others, a rustic house and a narrow path leading to a thick, pine woods. Further in the distance was a long gravel drive with a rambling barn, a truck filled with hay, and a horse standing stock-still, looking off in the distance. The composition was perfect. "Lovely," Po murmured. "Someday, Susan, I'm going to find me a spot like that." She gave her a quick hug, and hurried out the door.

Po drank her tea, but sleep came in starts and stops. Behind closed lids, she replayed her visit with Susan. There was something about the evening that tugged at her uncomfortably, pushed sleep back, far across the night. She wanted to get up out of bed and go back to her house and start the visit over, to see things she knew she was missing now in recollection.

The quilts were startling. The photographs, too.

But the most disconcerting, sleep-robbing thing of all was that there was something about Susan's house that made Po think she had been there before, seen it before. There was something about it that was disturbingly familiar. And it stood just beyond the reaches of her memory in a spot she couldn't quite see.

CHAPTER 22

Spinning Tops

Wednesday morning Po slept in, a luxury she didn't often afford herself but a necessity after a sleepless night. Finally, some time after eight o'clock, she pulled herself from beneath the covers and groped her way to the shower. Another hour or two would have suited her just fine, but not today. Today she needed to clear her head.

After feeding Hoover and opening the garage door so Peter could get the lawnmower out, Po called Kate. If Peter could cut the grass because he didn't have school, maybe

Kate was free, too.

"Parent-teacher conferences," Kate announced. "And the college is on mid-term break. God's in the heavens, all's right in the world."

"Well, almost," Po laughed. "I'm starving. Are you up for a plate of eggs at Marla's?"

"Have I ever said no to food?"

In twenty minutes, Po was seated at the front table in the middle of the bay window, her favorite spot on a sunny day. While sunlight beat down on the table, she could sit back and see the whole block: Max's empty office across the street; the parade of college kids biking and jogging and enjoying a week of freedom; shoppers moving in and out of the wine and cheese store, the bookstore. She saw Daisy standing in front of her store, staring at the window box. If she stared much harder, Po thought, it just might come tumbling down. And wouldn't that be good for everyone.

At the far corner she could just make out the corner of the quilt shop. She wondered if Susan was at work today. She awoke with the certain feeling that Susan had wanted to tell her something, something difficult, perhaps. Maybe something she couldn't put into words. Susan had kept their conversation last night on a safe plane, talking about art and tea and chicken soup. But beneath it all, Po still couldn't shake the discomforting feeling that either Susan or her house had a message for her. And it was having a hard time being delivered.

Outside the bay window, gusty winds blew the few remaining leaves across the street and flattened them against the window just beyond Po's reach. She hoped Peter wasn't having trouble mowing the lawn in this wind.

"There you are." Kate hurried over, bringing the sweet scent of lavender with her.

She kissed Po on the top of her head. "I ran into Leah when I parked my bike in the alley. She's coming in, too." Kate dropped her backpack on the floor and sat down. She leaned her elbows on the table and looked at Po carefully. Her brows pulled together. "Po, you're not sleeping."

"Not as much as I'd like. I think we are an inch away from putting all this tragedy behind us, Kate, and then that inch stretches out into a foot. And I can't get my arms around it anymore."

"I wonder if that's what Wesley felt like," Kate said, "reaching for those bills. P.J. said someone must have planted those there, knowing what a scavenger Wesley was and that he couldn't pass an open dumpster without a peek inside."

"That makes sense. I'm convinced that we're right about the blackmail."

Leah, carrying several shopping bags, made her way to their table and sat down. "I love mid-term break."

"So you're treating yourself."

"I went back to look at those paperweights, Po. They're beautiful."

"You bought one?" Po lifted her eyebrows.

"No," Leah laughed. "But I did get one of the less expensive versions that Mary carries in the small gift boutique."

"Like the one Wesley Peet swiped," Kate said.

Leah nodded.

They paused while the waitress took their order, then Leah

continued.

"Even the more inexpensive paper weights are quite beautiful. It's hard to tell the difference, in fact, unless you line them up side-by-side. Why he picked one of those to fling through Mary's window is a mystery. Wouldn't a rock have done the same job?"

"Hmm, good point," Po said, pondering the thought.

"I stopped in Ambrose and Jesse's for some cheese and to do a little snooping," Leah went on. "They have a big display of Chivas on that round rack in the middle of the store. Ambrose was adamant that he hadn't left a bottle outside the door to get Wesley drunk. Said it was the craziest thing he'd ever heard. Why use a Cadillac when a Chevy would do the same job? he said."

Why indeed, Po thought. Except the Rolls Royce would be irresistible. Fail-safe. If someone was determined to get Wesley woozy, that was the way to go. And it had been a pint bottle, enough to make him sloppy and weak, but not fall-down drunk so he wouldn't even see the dumpster or try to get the money. Whoever planned Wesley's murder was careful, exact. And capable of buying expensive whiskey and littering one hundred dollar bills on the floor of the dumpster.

"Did Ambrose say he'd sold any of that Scotch in the last couple days?" Po asked.

"He said of course he did. It was the world's most popular Scotch, or something to that effect."

"P.J. said they checked on that," Kate said. "I guess it is popular — for those who can afford it. Jesse gave P.J. a long list. And only credit card and check purchases will be recorded with names. I saw the first couple of names and remember one because it surprised me."

"Who?" Leah held a forkful of eggs in mid-air.

"Reverend Gottrey's wife ordered a bunch of liquor recently. And Chivas was on the list. They had a reception for the new church elders."

"And served liquor?" Po asked.

Kate nodded. "It was a fancy affair, I think, not at the church but at his home. They had elected three new elders — Mary Hill was one — and invited important people to greet the elders at a late-afternoon reception. Ambrose provided all the liquor and cheeses."

"Ambrose does a good business," Po said. "These murders don't seem to have harmed him at all."

"He seemed nervous, though," Leah said. "Edgy, as if he were afraid something was going to come back and bite him."

"I think everyone is nervous." Kate motioned to the young waitress for more coffee.

Outside the window, leaves continued to dance against the windowpane and the wind picked up, grabbing loose pieces of paper and chasing them across the street and into the curbs. Turmoil, Po thought. But surely it would all come together soon.

She listened to Kate and Leah's chatter with half an ear, her eyes watching the easy flow of people, back and forth across the street, stopping now and then to greet a friend or neighbor. Daisy was still outside her store. She stood in front of the boxes now with a small shovel in her hand, loosening the dirt. Po held back a smile, wondering what color of plastic tulip would be carefully patted into that rich, nourishing soil.

She looked across the street. Max's office looked so forlorn. Someone had mowed the small patch of grass in front. But the curtains were drawn and the steps leading up to the door were littered with leaves. People walked by and looked up, wondering if he'd come back. And probably wondering, too, how such a nice man had gotten mixed up in such a sordid mess as the Elderberry murders. The door to the office opened, and for a second, Po expected Max himself to hurry down the steps, his ever-present briefcase tucked under his arm. She squinted against the morning sun to see who'd be coming out of the small law office. A cleaning person, perhaps? But the man walking down the steps would never stoop to cleaning someone's office, at least not in his carefully pressed pants.

Looking to his left and then to his right, then scurrying down the steps — like the inept burglar in a Peter Sellers movie, Po thought — was Ambrose Sweet, a thick pile of papers tucked beneath his arm.

CHAPTER 23

End of the Day

After Leah and Kate left the cafe, Po hurried over to Ambrose's store and confronted him outright about what she'd seen, a decidedly foolish thing to have done, she thought later. Something Kate and Phoebe might have done.

But Ambrose had been cool and discreet.

Of course he'd been over at Max's, Ambrose told her. "Max was a friend, our attorney, and who in heaven's name do you think was mowing Max's lawn for him and picking up his newspapers while he has been so indisposed?"

Ambrose was so quick and articulate in his explanation that Po was held to uncharacteristic silence. She didn't for a minute believe him. But at a loss for words, she bought a bottle of sauvignon blanc, a hunk of Vermont white cheddar, and then hurried out of the store.

From Ambrose's shop, she walked slowly toward her car, her head full of unconnected facts and her heart heavy. There was a pall over the Elderberry shops, an invisible gray cloud. It was surely time for it to blow away. She put her packages in the back seat of her small Honda. Then, without conscious plan or careful thought, she drove across the river, through the west side of town, and out near the highway, where a lonely strip of warehouses stood along a wide street. Nearby was the garden supply store she went to every spring, and next to that, a tiny diner that had somehow lured Max Elliott into tragic danger.

Inside the diner Po found a small woman, perhaps seventy or so, behind a spotless Formica counter. A few workers in jeans and plaid shirts, probably taking an early lunch, lingered in a booth near the door, smoking cigarettes and talking.

"I told the police everything I know," the woman said, rubbing her hands on her apron nervously. "Mr. Max came here every single Thursday for twenty years. He never missed. If you know Mr. Max, you know he comes to Hedda's on Thursday."

Po looked around the restaurant. It was clean and simple. And, she suspected from the smells coming out of the kitchen, the food was probably wonderful. "He was your friend?" Po asked.

The woman nodded. "I had some legal problems a thousand years ago and went to one of them groups that helps you out. Max volunteered there, and he helped me. Then helped me get this restaurant. He never took a dime from me, so I insisted I feed him. And he came every Thursday without fail."

She smiled sadly and put her hands on the counter, looking off toward an empty booth that Po suspected would always be Max's.

"He loved my meatloaf, you know," Hedda said.

Po left Hedda's, then drove out of town, skirting the highway and turning onto a road that headed west, as far as the eye could see. Her head was swimming with thoughts of a kind man, who put a standing engagement with a lonely lady ahead of everything, even a meeting of Elderberry shopowners.

The town of Crestwood fell behind and in minutes Po was in the country, driving past farmland and wheat fields on a flat country road that stretched across the state like a long thin line. If you followed it far enough, you'd find yourself in the middle of the Kansas flint hills and rolling ranch lands. But Po didn't have to go that far to find what she needed to see.

Peter had just finished mowing the lawn and was putting the mower back in the garage when Po returned. The temperature had dropped to an uncomfortable chill. "The yard looks great, Peter," Po called to him. "I think you just made it before the first snow."

End of the Day

"My mom would be happy to hear that," Pete said. "She says I'm not ahead of anything."

"Well, you are in my book. We still have a deal for shoveling snow, ok?"

"Cool." Peter started to walk down the driveway, then stopped suddenly and turned around, walking back toward Po.

"I almost forgot. I found something weird in your backyard." He dug around in his pocket and pulled out a medallion with a dirty red ribbon dangling from it and handed it to her.

Po looked at it curiously. At first she didn't recognize the flat, dirty piece of metal that nearly filled her palm. "Where did you find this?"

"Behind that oak tree in the back of the yard. Back where Hoover buries his bones. Wasn't there last time I mowed, that I know for sure because I raked that whole area. Besides, it's big. I couldn't have missed it, and it's not dirty enough to have been there long."

"Well, thanks, Pete," she said absently, staring at it, her fingers rubbing off flakes of dry dirt and recognition falling on her like the night. She turned and walked through the back door, her heart lodged tightly against her ribs. She knew exactly what this was. Sam had started the tradition, and after he died, the new president continued it — giving honorary medallions to professors who had done exemplary jobs. They handed them out at commencement, one award each year. Po walked over to the sink and held it under running water, washing off the loose dirt.

She sat down at the table and rubbed it lightly with a soft rag, then slowly turned it over. A poem or saying was engraved on the back of each large medallion to make it personal and unique. Po pulled her glasses from her pocket and put them on. She recognized the poem. It was by Franz Boaz, and was one of Sam's favorites:

The woods were made for the hunters of dreams,
The brooks for the fishers of songs;
To the hunters who hunt for the gunless game,
The streams and the woods belong.

And she knew before she looked what initials she would find engraved beneath the poem — the initials of last June's faculty honoree: O.P.H. — Owen Patterson Hill.

Po looked down at Hoover. Her chest was tight. Sadness fell on her like a heavy wool cloak.

"Hoover," she said softly, "you shouldn't take things that don't belong to you."

And as the pieces of the puzzle finally began to fall into place, Po grabbed her jacket, put the medallion in her pocket, and flew out the back door and into the early darkness.

Susan was home and waiting for her when she pulled into the drive. "Selma called to see how I was. She told me you called to see if I was at the store today," she said quietly. "I figured you'd come back. Come in, Po."

Po followed her into the living room. A small light cast warm, yellow shadows about the room.

"My mom's in bed," Susan said. "It's okay to talk. You recognized the quilt, didn't you."

Po nodded. "Not for awhile, though. I went for a ride in the country today. I headed out that way without real thought. Then there it was."

Susan smiled softly. "Probably the only place in my life where I've been completely happy," she said.

"And then there was this." She handed Susan the medallion.

Susan gasped. "How did you get this?"

"I think Hoover stole it from your backseat the night you took me home. When I read the poem on the back, I remembered Owen's great love for his farm, and it all came into focus: the quilt, the black and white photographs. When I drove out there today, it all began to fit together."

Susan looked up. "I loved him, Po. More than anything in this world."

"I can see that, Susan. It's there in the quilt."

"That was our amazing, magical place." Her eyes filled with tears. "I took a class from Owen right before starting work at Selma's. It was complicated, Po. But not sordid, and believe it or not, his wife didn't care."

"No one knows what goes on between two people," Po began.

"But I know." Susan looked up. "Owen and Mary's marriage had been dead for a long time, Po, as self-serving and trite as that sounds. Mary would probably tell you herself if you asked her. She and Owen had separated in spirit years before. Mary had her church, Owen his work. They hadn't shared their life in any meaningful way for a long time. Mary didn't want a divorce because of the way it would look, so they just went their own ways. Then we met, and it changed things for him." Susan looked at the quilt again and the tears that had collected in her eyes began to fall.

"But I was ready to walk away from it, afraid it would

become a scandal and hurt someone, until . . ." Susan stopped for a minute and gathered her emotions.

"It was Max," she said finally, looking back at Po. "Dear Max. He convinced me not to leave Owen. He said Mary and Owen were deadening each other's life, and they'd both be happier apart. He was loyal to them both, you see. But he thought Mary was slipping into an unreal world and needed to face life. She wasn't speaking to Owen any longer, and was spending increasing amounts of time at the church, seeking their recognition and approval. She hated Owen. She only wanted his name and her good standing." The tears ran down her cheeks. Susan walked over to a roll-top desk. She pulled out a document and handed it to Po. "Max gave me this the day after Owen died."

Po read the legal document. It was the deed to Owen's farm, and ownership had been transferred to Susan Miller. "The farm is yours, Susan?"

"We were so happy there. We spent hours in the woods, hiking, riding horses."

"What have you done about this?" Po held up the deed. "Mary has given this property away."

"I haven't done anything. I don't want to cause any trouble, Po. I've lost Owen. I just want to know who did this horrible thing. Mary can give the land to the church if she wants." Susan managed a small smile, then added, "though Owen must be hollering in his grave over that. He was ready to cut off all donations to the church. He thought they'd given them plenty of money, and he had found other charities that were doing wonderful things for the homeless and children. Kids with no place to go after school. He wanted to help them for awhile, he said."

"And Mary?"

"And Mary, what?"

Susan and Po jerked around. Mary Hill stood in the front door, her lovely suit smooth and perfect, her hair pulled tightly back. She stood still and calm, a small antique pistol in her hand.

"Please," she said, "finish your conversation. I've only heard a little, but I'm terribly interested. I came here to settle a few things with Susan, but I got double my money's worth, Po. That's just fine."

Po didn't move. Her heart hammered inside her chest as she looked into the cold, glinting eyes of a woman who now seemed a stranger to her.

"Mary . . ." Susan started to move toward her.

"Sit," Mary said calmly. She looked around the room, the gun held steady. "Owen didn't put much money into this place, I see." Then she turned her attention to Po. "You probably didn't know he had a girlfriend, did you, Po? I encouraged it. It suited us nicely. As long as no one knew. No one could ever know." Her voice turned icy, and she turned and glared at Susan. "But you got uppity, didn't you? You were going to leave him. You awful woman, you!"

Po leaned forward. "Mary, you're not making sense."

The gun swung in her direction. "That's all you know, Po Paltrow. You and your Sam and your books and your friends. People think you're something. Well, I'm an elder at my church now. Did you know that? People look up to me. They respect me. They love me." She smiled, the same smile she had put in place to thank the Reverend Gottrey for making her an elder of the church, for the mayor when he gave her the citizen's award. It was a smile on a billboard — careful, perfect, empty.

"Of course they do, Mary." Po tried to rise in her chair but Mary pushed her back with a swing of her pearl-handled gun.

"But what do you think they would do if they knew my husband was going to cut off the funds to the church and divorce me? How would that look, Po? They don't make elders out of divorced women without money, ones whose husbands run off with cheap women." She stood very erect and pulled her thin brows together. "They'd be feeling sorry for me. I'd be the one they prayed for on Sundays. I'd be poor, divorced Mary Hill. People would come in my store and point at me. How would that look, Po?"

Mary's voice had risen so high that Po wouldn't have recognized it if Mary hadn't been standing in front of her, brandishing a gun.

"Mary, you have friends, no matter what. There's Max . . ."

"Max Elliott is a fool," she said sharply. "He agreed with Owen. Always, always. And he had the nerve to come to me at the store and show me her name on that deed." Mary pointed at Susan, the tip of the gun inches from her face. "Foolishness. It belongs to the church, not Owen's lover. Max was foolish and fickle. He said he was there to help me, and he wiped away my tears that day. And the whole time, he planned to see that she got the farm. He got what he deserved, foolish man."

"But how did you . . ." Po started. Then she glanced at the photograph of the farm, and spotted the truck in front of the barn. A beat-up old truck that Owen used to lug around his fence posts and fertilizer. Mary. She'd taken that truck.

"I drove that truck right over Max," she said proudly, following Po's gaze. "He used to tell Owen and me about that old woman — how he used to eat her meatloaf every Thursday in that empty dismal restaurant. Such a foolish man. He has never been made an elder, you know."

Po thought back to the day she and Leah had seen Mary crying in the store —- the shadowy figure holding her, the crumbled paper in her hand when she had hurried down the street.

"And Wesley must have seen you, maybe the night you killed Owen?" Po asked.

"That snoop saw everything. He knew about Susan. She and Owen used to meet in the quilt store sometimes. In Selma's back room. She was there that night after the meeting. They were making plans. I knew it. Wesley knew it, too. He sneaked around, drinking his liquor, making his slurs. Silly, useless man. I paid him off — a truck. But he kept wanting more."

"The paperweight?"

Mary laughed. It was a hollow, eerie sound.

"A fake. I told him he could sell it someday for thousands of dollars, but he had to wait for the value to go up. Damn fool took it directly to a pawn shop, of all things. And they told him it wasn't real. Of course I would never give that ugly man a Perthshire."

"And us, Mary? Susan and me?"

"I stopped by Selma's today and saw that chart you had put together. Those other girls won't figure it out. They think Ambrose or Gus, maybe, or that crazy Daisy Sample. But you I don't trust." She pointed the gun at Susan. "And you? You are the cause of it all. He wanted to marry you!"

"Mary, the church can keep the farm," Susan said, but she realized Mary wasn't listening.

Po had seen the shadows fall over the windows behind Mary, then disappear. She saw the black hat and jeans, the sunny hair. And Kate, tall and gangly. Maggie and a flash of red hair. Selma, bless her heart. Leah brought up the rear and disappeared just before Mary looked out the window, then back to the two women in front of her.

"Mary, it won't work," Po said. She watched carefully and wondered if there had been other times, other instances, when she should have noticed the grave imbalance in Mary Hill.

Mary's eyes were beginning to glaze over. She tried to focus. "Of course it will work. I am a very smart, very well-loved woman. I'm an elder in my church, you know." She smiled brightly.

The door opened so quietly that Po thought for a moment Mary didn't hear it. But then she turned, staring straight into Phoebe Mellon's blazing blue eyes.

What happened in the next 60 seconds was a scene straight out of a Charlie's Angels flick, as Phoebe described it to anyone who would listen.

As Mary spun around, Po raised one strong, well-exercised arm and snapped Mary's slender wrist up higher than her head. The small pearl handled gun flew out of her hand, straight up into the air.

Eight heads followed its flight.

Mary lurched for control. And at that precise moment, the law of gravity kicked in and the gun fell soundly and surely into Phoebe's waiting palm.

"Yahoo!" she screamed.

Mary, her face bright red, moved toward the door. Maggie and Leah and Kate, their legs stretched wide, blocked the way.

In the distance, sirens screamed their way through the quiet neighborhood.

"P.J.," Kate beamed. And then she grabbed Po and hugged her close, tears streaming down her face.

EPILOGUE

Joy Bells

It was springtime when the Queen Bees finished Selma's Crystal Star quilt. By then the story had grown old, told and retold so many times that sometimes even the Queen Bees got mixed up on what really happened.

The papers said the police had found sound, incriminating evidence that Mary Hill had murdered her husband and Wesley, including a receipt for the hundred-dollar bills and the pint of Scotch. She'd thrown the rock that crushed

Owen's skull into Hans Broker's backyard, where Hans had found it and used it to replace an old one in his small rock garden. Sparky finally unburied it, revealing the bloody edge. And the beat-up old truck, Owen's own farm vehicle, had fingerprints galore, the paper said.

As for the final capture, Selma herself had played an important role. She'd been suspicious for weeks that Owen and Susan had a thing for each other. "You can't be around it," she admitted, "and not have a feeling." But it was Susan's business, and she left it alone, trusting that Susan would do the right thing.

But the day of the phone calls asking for Susan's address — first Po, then Mary — worried her no end. And when Kate and Maggie came in with the news that Mary had bought the whiskey, and Leah remembered seeing the old truck out at Owen's farm, they began to put the pieces together. Phoebe drew crossing lines on the white easel paper, and bingo — they had it.

Kate called P.J. to tell him their news and promised him they'd stay put. Then they flipped the closed sign on the front door of the shop, piled into Selma's car, and the rest was Crestwood history.

Now, at last, after countless Saturdays spent sewing and not sleuthing, the anniversary quilt was finished, just in time for the fiftieth anniversary of the Quilt Shop. But they decided to have a private unveiling first, just the Queen Bees, and family, of course.

Susan insisted it be out at her farm. She had moved her mother and a nurse into the guesthouse behind the main house, and she lived alone in the spacious home that Owen had loved. Today the house was ready for her first guests: the ladies she trusted with her life.

Po and Kate busied themselves in the kitchen, putting out champagne glasses, small plates for the cake, and silverware and napkins. The others prepared the quilt in the great room, attaching it to a rod and covering it with a satin sheet. They had all seen it completed, of course, except for Selma, who had been excluded from the final binding.

"We're ready," Leah called out from the big room, as Owen had called it. Kate and Po gathered up the glasses and came into the room. Po stood on the porch and called to the others.

Jimmy and the twins, walking as straight as little rulers now, came in from feeding the horses, and P.J. poured champagne all around. Tim lit a fire in the fireplace to take the bite out of the air, then stood beside Leah while Po took center stage.

"We've so much to celebrate," Po said. Everyone gathered around her. "First, to Life . . ."

The clink of glasses echoed in the air. "Here, here!"

"And healing," Po said. They turned as one and lifted their glasses to the small quiet man sitting off to the side. Max was in a wheelchair now, and recovering every day. Po had been there visiting the day he woke up. After three months in a coma, he had rolled his head to the side of the pillow, looked Po in the eye, and said in a strong, clear voice: "Po, where's my meatloaf? Food's terrible here."

Ambrose and Jesse had helped build a ramp for Max's office after he was released from rehab, and he managed to show up for a couple of hours each day. In exchange, Max was helping them clean up all the discrepancies in their books that he and Owen had discovered. It was a second chance for them, designed to keep the IRS at bay — and Max would help them do it.

Po lifted her glass and met Max's eyes. She smiled as glasses were raised in his direction.

"To Max." Voices chimed and glasses clinked.

"And to friendship," Po said, as the billowy drape fell off the quilt, and the room fell silent

Selma sat on the couch, right in front of the Queen Bees' dazzling star quilt. Her eyes were moist as she looked at the millions of tiny stitches that held it together, the hours of chatter and tears and friendship that bound it as tightly as the deep purple binding.

In the center of the quilt was Susan's contribution: magnificent beaded clusters of deep blue-black elderberries, their appliquéd stems standing out in relief.

As Selma reached out and touched it, Susan walked over and planted a big kiss on her cheek. Susan had begun teaching new quilting techniques in Selma's back room — beading and ribbon appliqué and photograph transfers. The shop was alive with new art, and a public television station had even included the class, and the Queen Bees, in a documentary for public television.

The attention and the classes had brought new customers and revenue streams to Selma's store, and the fiftieth anniversary was truly a celebration. The Elderberry neighborhood had taken on new life as it shook itself free of fear. The antique store was in new hands, and the young couple who bought it thought brick sidewalks were terribly dangerous. They also believed antiques should be seen, and had brightened up the store, adding a skylight in the very center. Daisy had finally agreed to an anger management class, and Selma went with her every Tuesday to make sure she didn't skip. Leah and Susan helped her fix and paint the old window boxes, and at Christmas time, she filled them with tiny live pine trees and dozens of sparkling lights.

Gus and his wife Rita were helping plan Selma's anniversary celebration, even inviting the mayor to make a toast. And Marla's ovens had been humming for two weeks straight as she baked enough anniversary desserts to line Elderberry Road from one end to the other.

"A good day," Po said to Kate as the evening at the farm wound down. They were standing side-by-side at Susan's sink, their arms up to elbows in hot, soapy water.

Kate nodded. She shoved up the sleeve of her white blouse, leaving clusters of soap bubbles standing on her arm.

Po looked over at her goddaughter. Good day, for sure. And a good life. She lifted her arm from the sink of suds and pulled Kate close. Her eyes looked across the window and toward the sun sinking slowly behind the woods.

"See, Meg?" she said silently to herself. "I promised — and she's still safe. Still sassy, still our girl. Stay tuned, dear friend."

About the Author

Sally Goldenbaum is the author of over two dozen published novels, including a mystery written with Nancy Pickard. She is an editor at a veterinary publishing company, mother of three grown children, and lives in Prairie Village, Kansas, with her husband, Don, two dogs, and a cat.

How To Make The Crystal Star
8" Block

From the background fabric, cut four squares using template A and four triangles using template C.

From the medium fabric, cut 12 triangles using template B.

From the light fabric, cut on square using template D.

Sew a medium B triangle to two sides of each C triangle making a flying geese unit. Make four of these units.

Sew a medium B triangle to each side of the D square.

Sew an A square to opposing sides of two of the flying geese units. This will make the top and bottom row of the block.

Now sew a flying geese unit to either side of the center square in a square block

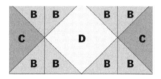

Sew the top and bottom rows to the center row to complete the block.

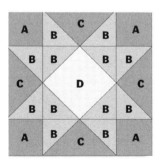

CRYSTAL STAR

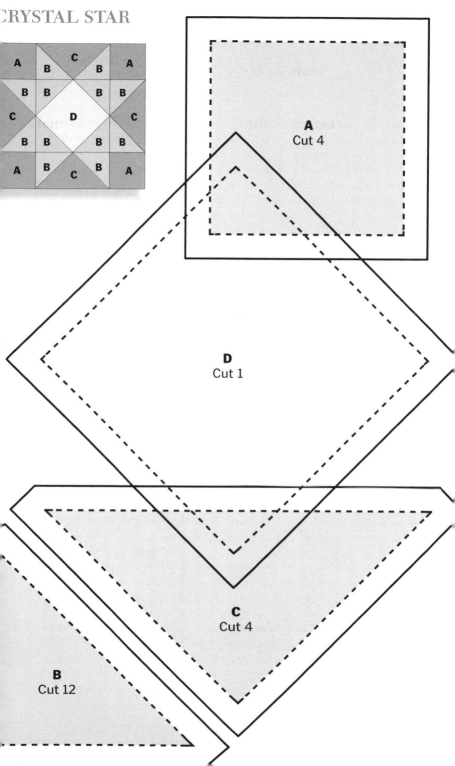

A	B	C	B	A
B	B		B	B
C		D		C
B	B		B	B
A	B	C	B	A

A
Cut 4

D
Cut 1

C
Cut 4

B
Cut 12

Great Quilt Titles from Kansas City Star Books

Star Books specializes in quilting books inspired by the more than 1,000 quilt patterns that prairie women submitted to The Star from the 1920s through the 1960s.

The books feature both prior patterns and many new designs produced by some of quilting's best designers.

Visit www.TheKansasCityStore.com or www.PickleDish.com, or call us toll-free at 1-866-834-7467.

Come see why quilters worldwide enjoy the books of Kansas City Star Quilts!

Titles available:

Star Quilts II: More Kansas City Star Quilts
By The Kansas City Star

Star Quilts III: Outside the Box
By Edie McGinnis

Star Quilts IV: Prairie Flower: A Year on the Plains
By Barbara Brackman

Star Quilts V: The Sister Blocks
By Edie McGinnis

Star Quilts VI: Kansas City Quiltmakers
By The Kansas City Star

Star Quilts VII: O' Glory: American Quilt Blocks from The Kansas City Star
By Edie McGinnis

Star Quilts VIII: Hearts and Flowers: Hand Appliqué from Start to Finish
By Kathy Delaney

Star Quilts IX: Celebration of American Life: Appliqué Patterns Honoring a Nation and Its People
By Barb Adams and Alma Allen

Star Quilts X: Roads and Curves Ahead
By Edie McGinnis

Star Quilts XI: A Heartland Album: More Techniques in Hand Appliqué
By Kathy Delaney

Star Quilts XII: Quilting a Poem: Original Designs Inspired by America's Most Beloved Poets
By Francis Kite and Debra Rowden

Star Quilts XIII: Carolyn's Paper-Pieced Garden: Historic Patterns for Miniature and Full-Size Quilts
By Carolyn Cullinan McCormick

COMING FALL 2003:

Women of Grace and Charm: Applique Patterns Honoring a Generation
By Barb Adams and Alma Allen

Baskets of Treasures: Designs Inspired by Life Along the River
By Edie McGinnis

Heart & Home: Unique American Women and the Houses that Inspire
By Kathy Schmitz

Friendships in Bloom: Round Robin Quilting

Visit us at www.TheKansasCityStore.com or www.PickleDish.com!